3-11-97

THE
DARK SIDE
OF THE GAME

Tim Green is also the author of three novels
based on his NFL playing experiences:

RUFFIANS
TITANS
OUTLAWS

THE ____
DARK SIDE
OF THE GAME

My Life in the NFL

TIM GREEN

WARNER BOOKS

A Time Warner Company

Copyright © 1996 by Tim Green
All rights reserved.

Warner Books, Inc., 1271 Avenue of the Americas, New York, NY 10020
W A Time Warner Company

Printed in the United States of America
First Printing: August 1996
10 9 8 7 6 5 4

Library of Congress Cataloging-in-Publication Data

Green, Tim
    The dark side of the game : my life in the NFL / Tim
Green.
        p.   cm.
    Includes index.
    ISBN 0-446-52033-0
    1. National Football League.   2. Football—Social aspects—United
States.   I. Title.
GV955.5.N35G74   1996
796.332'02'02—dc20   95-51000
                                                        CIP

Book design by Giorgetta Bell McRee

This book is for my remarkable wife, Illyssa, whose unending patience and love make every day feel like a championship victory. And for Stu Lisson, who taught me how to look at the world like an artist from the time I was six years old.

ACKNOWLEDGMENTS

I would like to thank my editor, Rick Wolff, for his tireless work on this book. I would like to say that *The Dark Side of the Game* was my own idea, but it was really his. The check's in the mail.

Also, thanks to Rob McMahon for his careful reading of the manuscript and his helpful ideas.

I must say that writing about sports is something I have done before. The people who helped me develop this craft are Mark Schramm and Tom Goldman, my editors and friends at National Public Radio, and Bud Poliquin, my editor at *The Syracuse Herald Journal*.

Thanks to my parents, Dick and Judy Green, for never missing a Little League football game.

Thanks to Ed Goren, executive producer of FOX Sports, and David Hill, president of FOX Sports, for giving me a chance, and to Tracy Dolgin, FOX Sports' executive VP for marketing, for going above and beyond to spread the word about my books.

Special thanks to Jerry Glanville, Matt Millen, John Madden, Terry Bradshaw, and Jimmy Johnson, who shared with me their stories and insights into the NFL.

Finally, I want to thank all my football coaches. They taught me the essential elements of the game, and life. In particular: Ron Kelly, my Little League coach and the guy who taught me to dream; Ron Osinski, my mentor, high school football coach, and English teacher, who taught me about the common denominator between books and sports—passion; Dick MacPherson, my head coach at Syracuse University, who taught me how to prioritize my life; Mike Woicik, for his tireless hours with me in the weight room; George Mangicaro and Buzz White, for sticking by me through thick and thin; and finally, George O'Leary, who coached me in high school at Liverpool, in college at Syracuse University, and who advised me while I was in the NFL even though he was coaching for the Chargers at the time, for teaching me to bring the dark side of myself to every down of football I ever played. I hope I made you proud.

CONTENTS

AUTHOR'S NOTE

Billions of dollars are spent each year in this country and around the world by people who want to absorb the essence of the game of football. People talk about it, watch it, read about it, play it, and wager their hard-earned dollars on its outcomes. In short, there is an obsession with the game and the personalities that surround it. I think the reason is simple. Like our society, football is fast paced and violent. The stakes are high, fame and fortune, the American dream. Losers are carted off the field or forced into retirement with battered and mangled bodies, not unlike the gladiators of old. It is the primal connection with physical battle confined only by the rules of sport, testing athletes on every level—speed, intelligence, quickness, strength, endurance, grace, and mental toughness—that makes football so popular. Still, very few know what it really *feels* like.

The NFL is bent on maintaining an image of pristine competition, a rugged figure skating championship if you will, something the family can enjoy. Football is that, complete with the banners and the drama and the heroes, but it's also much more. Football encompasses the tragedies of modern-day life as well as the comedies. There are as many things that go on inside the world of the NFL that are heartwarming as there are horrifying. To date, I believe only two types of books have been written about the game of football: laudatory celebrations of great players and great seasons, or malcontent grumblings by those who were ground up in the maw of the league and spit out. In either case, only one facet of the experience was examined.

Because I have lived through it, I know that playing in the NFL lives up to the childhood dreams of an eight-year-old boy, secretly clutching the golden figure of a Pop Warner championship trophy under his bedcovers as he drifts off to sleep. I also know that to play in the NFL, one must endure or succumb to pressures bent on compromising the soul in ways that would have made Daniel Webster shudder. From one perspective football players look like a herd of bumbling morons, whose childish understanding of the real world can split your side. From another perspective they are the last remnant of the Arthurian knights. And, like all celebrities, they are largely misunderstood and grossly stereotyped.

I have no personal agenda in this project. I have no desire to indict anyone or anything. I don't care to make myself, or anyone, out to be better or worse than they really are. Rather, I hope to open a window for people so that they can at last have an intimate look inside the world of the NFL, to see the Tiffany fixtures, and the plumbing as well.

THE DARK SIDE OF THE GAME

THE DREAM

When I meet people for the first time and they learn that I played for eight years in the NFL, their eyes glaze over with that faraway look of a person dreaming about what he'll do if he wins the lottery. Millions of people dream about playing in the NFL, and I can say with all honesty that indeed it is an enviable path to have traveled.

There's the money, that's the obvious thing. Even the average player in the NFL earns in two years what it takes most of the rest of the country to earn *in a lifetime*. I remember thinking about that at the moment when I signed my first NFL contract. I thought of my own dad coming home, tired and worn from working and struggling, day after day, throughout my entire life, to earn what I would make for a signing bonus with the mere flourish of a pen. I was a twenty-two-year-old college senior. So, in a way, being an NFL player, where the average guy will earn two and a half million dollars in his career, is just like winning a lottery. But it's more.

There's the fame. I'm not just talking about making a few extra thousand dollars endorsing a box of cereal or

1

a car dealership. Fame is more than that. Fame is about autographing one of your playing cards for a little kid in the hospital. Your heart aches like a broken bone when you walk into his room and see the tubes and the scars and his pale sickly skin. You say hello, then you sign your card and hand it to him. His face bursts open like a brilliant spring flower with that pure unadulterated joyful grin that only kids can have. That's fame. It's liquid, and when you have it, it drips off your fingertips and flows from your words, splashing onto other people and making them happy just because you're there. There is no feeling like that, and that too is part of the dream.

There's the satisfaction. You have to work hard to get to the NFL. It's not like some other sports. No one gets there on raw talent alone. There are too many obstacles and too many other players, violent and vicious, waiting to take you down. In that way, it's like a game of chess. Even the lowest pawn, in the right position, can take out the king and end the game. If you're the fastest kid in the state of Texas destined to be the next Jerry Rice, you may never get there because some gap-toothed duck-footed linebacker from Odessa laid you out in the fourth quarter of a 67–0 game and ended your career before it ever really got started. There isn't a player in the NFL who hasn't endured the agonies of grueling physical work and injury. Getting to the NFL is like climbing Mt. Everest, there's a distinct pleasure in just the knowledge that you're one of the few who ever made it.

Then there's the thrill. Imagine getting to the summit of that same mountain, only now, when your head breaks through the clouds, surrounding you on every side are seventy-five thousand people screaming—for you. When you run out onto the field of an NFL stadium, that energy from the crowd surges into your veins with a jolt like it came from a giant capacitor. It feels like you might just get lifted right up off your feet and zip off into the sky like a spinning Chinese bottle rocket. You don't though; you stay right there and feel the energy as it continues to flow through you. Then you get to play, and if you thought that crowd was with you during introductions, just try sacking the quarterback or scoring a touchdown. If you're winning, and you're making big plays, you can ride the energy of that crowd like a wave.

It's not just an adrenaline rush. People talk about adrenaline rush all the time like it's a big deal. An adrenaline rush is what you get when you have a traffic accident or a shouting match with your boss. When you play in an NFL game it's more like some mad scientist bottled up the adrenaline, mixed in a bolt of lightning, harnessed a nuclear flash, then shot the whole thing directly into your aorta. If someone talks about an adrenaline rush, don't pay any attention. An adrenaline rush is like a bowl of cold soup compared to the charge you feel playing in an NFL game.

Fame and fortune, satisfaction and thrills, that's why people dream about playing in the NFL and they're right. Hell, I still dream that dream, even though I already did it. I work for FOX now, broadcasting games, and the truth is, I can't go onto the field before a game, to talk with players and coaches as they're making their last-minute preparations, without daydreaming about being back there again. I have this little fantasy that one time I'll be down there thirty minutes before kickoff in my jacket and tie and Dan Reeves will put his hand on my shoulder and say in that Georgia drawl of his, "Tim, Corey Miller just twisted his ankle in warm-ups. I know you've been out of it a little while, but we could sure use you today."

I can't help it. I'm like most red-blooded American

males. I wish I could live that dream for the rest of my days. The only thing you should know though, is that like almost everything else, there's a dark side. There are things that go on during the other three hundred and forty-nine days of the year when you're not playing a game, even things that go on during the game, on the sidelines, and in the locker room, that take their toll on the human body and spirit. Yes, the truth is, like most things in this life, there is a price and it must be paid . . .

The BLESTO Combines:
Welcome to the Big Leagues

Imagine being told to strip to your shorts. You stand in a line of other men, also almost naked. The floor is cold. It's concrete. Your feet are clammy. You can smell the pungent sour odor of your own armpits; it's that nervous smell. The line advances slowly toward the front of the room where, one by one, the men are weighed and measured with the cold efficiency of a slaughterhouse. Sloppy-looking overweight men in their forties and fifties sit stuffed into high school desk-chairs jotting furiously as the lab-coated technicians bark out the exact heights and weights of their subjects. You wonder about your own height and weight and how two more inches and twenty more pounds could be worth millions of dollars to you right now, but it's too late for that. Your craftier counterparts have been shooting up steroids for months to ensure not only the absolute maximum body weight, but strength and speed as well.

It's your turn, finally, and you step up onto a raised platform for all to see. The glaring men handling you like a quartered slab on a hook are pencil-necks in lab coats, men whom you wouldn't make room for at the bar under normal circumstances. After they announce your specific measurements, you're told to step down off the meat scale and proceed to the next station. It's through a rust-pocked gray steel door. You enter another room, this one smaller than the last, and darker. The direct spot lighting of a video camera nearly blinds you with its white, purple-edged light.

"Walk to the end of the line," someone from behind the light and camera says, "then stop at the end, and when I tell you, you'll turn around and walk back."

"Huh?" That's what you say. It sounds stupid, but who could blame you. It's hard to understand why the scions of the NFL would fly you halfway across the country just to get you in your shorts and videotape you walking up and down the length of a yellow line. Anyway, that's what you do and when you're done you proceed to yet another station.

The morning flies by. Before it's over, you've bench-pressed two hundred and twenty-five pounds over and over again until your arms turned to jelly and two lab coats had to step up to keep the weight from crushing your neck, you've run a forty-yard dash, vertical-jumped, long-jumped, and done several other unintelligible and inexplicable agility drills that in theory tell the men watching and timing you how good a football player you can really be. In reality, 90 percent of it doesn't mean a damn thing, but hey, coaches and scouts have to have something to do with themselves in the off-season and everyone these days is scared as hell to make a draft decision based solely on what kind of football player you appear to be.

After you've jumped and twisted and hurried and scurried like a rat in a cheese maze, it's time for the real fun to begin. It's time for your physical examination. You are mercifully loaded up with the other players onto a bus instead of a cattle truck and transported to a local hospital that has the necessary gizmos to further scrutinize what you once thought was your own body. It's on the bus ride that you get to think about why the hell you're here in the first place. It all seems so, so crazy. The answer is easy.

It's a badge of honor to get invited to The Combines. It tells you basically that someone out there cares enough about you as a player to take a closer look. If you don't get invited to The Combines, your odds of getting drafted or signed as a free agent in the upcoming NFL draft are microscopic.

You're no dummy; you know The Combines are the gateway to the NFL. Okay, they're degrading. But they can't be that bad. Every year the three hundred or so best college football players show up like migratory birds. Instinct, not reason, tells them to fly in the face of this storm of humiliation and degradation. It's like nobody has a choice. Oh, there are a few stories about guys in the past who forwent the opportunity. They got left by the wayside. There were always plenty of others to step up and take their places.

You look down at your hand. The ink from the fat black indelible marker where they wrote on you has leaked into the minuscule dermal canals giving you an idea of the unsightly leather pattern of your skin. What they have written is a number. You stop and think about how no one has called you by your name so far today, but instead by the number that matches the one on the back of your hand, which also of course matches the number on your official NFL shirt and gym shorts. You don't just feel like a number, you've become one.

When you get to the hospital, you're herded with the others into a long hallway to wait. Chairs line the way and at the end of the corridor is a door. A woman pops her head out the door every so often and beckons to the body filling the seat nearest the door. In the true spirit of the whole thing, the masses have somehow determined that the correct way to proceed is for all forty remaining bodies to lift their carcasses up, only to drop them immediately in the remaining empty seat. It's a truncated and ridiculous version of musical chairs without the music. At that rate, you will get up and sit down seventeen times before you are beckoned. You revolt. You decide to sit and not move. You'll wait for ten or so spaces to open up before you shuffle on down.

When four empty chairs are between you and the next guy, those behind you start to shift uncomfortably in their seats. Someone is not obeying the rules. That's not a good thing. You start to feel like the grandpa snaking through the mountains on a single-lane highway with twenty cars crawling up his back because he's going five miles under the speed limit. You surrender and take up your role in the mindless shuffle. Despite your sense of the absurdity, you feel much better.

As you sit, you notice a man working the crowd. He has a tape measure and a caliper. He is measuring the diameter of everyone's skulls and the circumferences of their fists. The guy next to you leans over and says that he heard some teams can tell how long you're likely to play in the league by inserting those very measurements into a scientific formula. You doubt this, but he seems to believe and you decide not to burst his bubble. Soon the man measures your skull and your hand. You peer into his eyes; he too seems to believe that these measurements are important.

When your turn finally arrives you see that the room you've been waiting to enter is something like a bazaar. There are ten attractions, and you have to go to each one. They give you little stickers and when you get one little sticker from each attraction, you get to leave. You thank the woman who has called you by your number and given you your folder to collect the stickers with. You turn, searching the large festive room for the smallest queue. It seems that this is the dental station. You sit on a stool and a man who you hope is a human dentist pulls back your lips to inspect your gums and teeth. He talks to himself and records what he says with a little Dictaphone. He notes the fillings in the back, but your teeth, and more importantly, your gums are good. He puts a little blue sticker on your folder and you move on.

Seven of the ten attractions are set up in little tents, separated from the din by heavy felt drapes. The lines for these are long, but when you get inside you are rewarded with the intimate setting of an examination table surrounded by a dozen or so doctors and trainers. You get up onto the table with a nervous giggle. They ask you questions about old injuries you had in college. You try to lie and say there weren't any. You don't want to be perceived as damaged goods. They've got you though. In the corner is a computer-literate trainer from one of the teams who is banging away and extracting your complete medical history, electronically preserved from somewhere in your past. Some of the things he pulls up you forgot about yourself, a broken finger, a bruised thigh. You had no idea they could get this information, so you come clean and admit that all your old injuries really exist.

You are a liar though and they all know it, so they start to poke you and pull at your limbs, twisting and testing for old weaknesses that may still exist. Someone grabs at your ribs and you jump.

"Does that hurt?" a gruff voice asks.

"No," you say ashamedly, "it tickles."

Hurumpfff.

By the time the front of your folder is dotted with ten stickers your joints ache as if you've just walked away from a brutal contest on the football field. There are other things to do in the hospital, but they are nothing more than anyone would have to endure during a thorough physical exam. No team wants to buy into a health risk, and if you've got a congenital heart problem or high blood pressure, your stock in the upcoming draft will drop. This makes sense to you. You wouldn't want to invest a million dollars in a sick race horse, why should they do so in a sick player?

The last task before you go home is an intelligence test. There are fifty questions and you have a limited amount of time to get through them all. Some of the highest scores you've heard of are in the mid-thirties. Others are fortunate that you get a point for filling in your name. You wonder if they take points off your intelligence score for the simple fact that you are here. That would make sense. It really doesn't matter though; you know that this is the least important test of the day. Some of the biggest NFL contracts have been awarded to the people who have scored two, three, and four on this exam. Still, you want to do well. It's a matter of pride. You still have your pride, don't you?

TRAINING CAMP

Every summer during my NFL career, without fail, someone would ask me, "I'll bet you're looking forward to the season."

"Yeah," I'd say, but I never really meant it.

No player in their right mind could look forward to the NFL season when training camp looms before it. To the fan, it's just preseason, an amusing time when teams get to travel around the world and play games just for the fun of it. But while everyone else is having barbecues and picnics in the month of August, NFL players are sweating, and bleeding, and hurting. To an NFL player, August means training camp, and there's nothing fun about it.

The days begin at seven and if you're lucky your last meeting is over by nine at night. Mixed in that full schedule are two of the most grueling practice sessions imaginable. The pounding your body takes during a day of these sessions can only be duplicated if you've been in a car wreck that you were lucky to walk away from. You know, when the next day your body hurts

11

everywhere? Well that's training camp, only you feel that way day in and day out for a month.

Of course all of this is even worse if you're a rookie. Besides the bruised body and somber spirits, rookies have to face humiliation and frustration. They are no longer the star of the team as they were in college. Hazing is an established tradition in the NFL. In Atlanta, rookies' heads were Mohawked or charitably shaven. Each had to take his turn atop the dinner table to sing amidst spirited heckling.

Short of the Mojave Desert, places like Atlanta, New Orleans, Tampa Bay, and Miami have to be the worst place in the world to have to go through two-a-days. As if it's not enough to need hot tubs and anti-inflammatory drugs just to get your broken body through the day, guys on those teams also have heat. I'm talking about ninety-five on the average, with humidity that makes it feel like a hundred and ninety-five.

The heat of training camp used to leave me fantasizing on the steamy field. Standing there between plays, head pounding, swimming in my own sweat, I'd think of the cool upstate New York lake on which I now live year-round. I could actually feel myself plunging into the clear green water, satiating my thirst with big gulps as I'd swim to the surface. A day never went by that I didn't wish I was there instead of training camp.

The heat is worse for the big linemen though, those three-hundred-pounders (I was a lean two-hundred fifty). Oh, they can get through practice, but after the bone-crunching sessions come the wind sprints. That's when we'd lose our three-hundred-pound friends to the heat. You could see them starting to fade, running slower and slower, huffing and puffing ever more acutely, until at last, almost mercifully, over they'd go like a water buffalo shot through the head. Trainers would appear like carrion fowl, and roll them off to the sideline so the rest of us could continue to run. The gasping giants would quickly be packed in ice, right there on the grass. The mounds of cool cubes were always a temptation for the rest of us to go down as well, even though we didn't.

Without doubt, the only good thing about training camp was when it was finally over.

ROOKIES IN SHORTS

Nothing is more meaningless in the game of NFL football than minicamps. Every spring, we get to hear how wonderful the new crop of rookies look in their shorts and jerseys. It's a joke. The things that go on in minicamp, running around, grunting and groaning, and slapping each other's hands, have nothing to do with the real thing in the fall.

I remember my second and third years in the league. I didn't know any of this. I would stand there during camp, watching the new rookies with my eyes agog. They always looked good. They were fresh and healthy and spirited beyond belief. They ran and snorted and tore up the turf in a way that made me worry for my job.

The veteran players who I was now good friends with laughed at me when I would worry out loud.

"Shorts mean nothing," they'd say. "Wait until the pads go on. These rookies won't know what hit them."

And it was true. What had become second nature to me, the speed, the violence, the intensity of contact in the NFL, would overwhelm almost every rookie. No

14

matter how good they looked in shorts, they were always in for a rude awakening come the beginning of camp. So the next time you see or read about some rookie in shorts and how good he looks during mini-camp in May or June? Don't buy it. You know better. Nothing counts in the NFL until the pads go on and the fire is live.

WHY TRAINING CAMP
IS FOOLISH

Sometimes we do things in life just because that's the way they've always been done. People used to think sitting in the sun was good for you, so they did. Now we know that it can kill you, but still, it's hard to convince people in our society to change. Things seem to change slowly in the world of the NFL, even slower than the world without. For years, people knew eating steaks didn't help you perform better on the field, but steaks were stuffed into football players on a regular basis until just recently. For years, it was proven that athletes needed water to perform at optimum levels, yet in football it was a long time before the opposite idea, that it was good to toughen players by not giving them water during practice or a game, was eradicated. Training camp is one of those anachronisms, a dinosaur that simply refuses to die. I don't think you could convince any player in the NFL that it is necessary to beat his brains out for five weeks in the August heat to prepare for an NFL season. Players spend their entire off-seasons training with weights to maximize their strength and body weight, only to see both eroded during camp.

A typical day of training camp goes like this: Players are usually up by seven o'clock. They eat a quick breakfast and get to the training room to get ankles taped for practice and get treatment for their existing injuries if necessary. By the time players have their bodies taped and padded up, it's usually around eight-thirty and time to get out on the field. Practice typically goes for about three hours. That includes some kind of conditioning in the last twenty minutes of the session, usually running sprints. With the heat, the hitting, the running, and the stress of coaches screaming, and players crashing into you from every direction, by the end of these three hours, you feel like you're ready for a two-week vacation in the Caribbean, but the day has just begun.

Weight lifting after the morning practice isn't an everyday thing, but at least three days a week you'd better be in there, or you'll be as weak as a water-logged worm by September. After lifting and a shower, there's lunch. Many players, dehydrated and exhausted, have to fight the urge to skip the meal and get right to their bunks. The body must have fuel for the afternoon session and a replenishment of potassium to avoid severe cramping. Many teams will have meetings now with individual position coaches to watch the film of the morning's practice. Almost every facet of practice is captured on film, so every mistake is relived under the scrutiny of a bellowing coach. It's rarely a pleasurable experience.

When the midday meetings are over, with the exception of the kickers and some quarterbacks, most players will try to sleep, or at least relax for an hour in their rooms. Some teams, like the Falcons, are lucky. They stay in hotels where comfortable double beds and air-conditioning make it easier to rest. Others stay in dorm rooms at remote college locations. They have to rely on portable fans to cool them and total exhaustion to get any rest in their sagging single dormitory bunks. This hour of rest is the shortest period of the day.

Many players, anxious to the point of distraction in their hostile surroundings, lose themselves in the midday soap operas on television. Along with millions of housewives, these macho, world-class athletes escape their own reality for a few brief minutes in the swirl of an emotional turmoil of a much more innocuous sort. If you are an Atlanta Falcon during training camp and you don't follow *The Young and the Restless*, you might be left out of the locker room conversation during the afternoon. If you're one of the lucky ones who can sleep during this hour, your eyes seem to close for nothing more than seconds before the alarm goes off. Your sleep is so deep that you often awake not knowing where you are. The bumps, scrapes, and bruises covering your entire body like a plague of boils soon remind you of exactly where you are and that it's time to get retaped and dressed for the afternoon practice.

In effect, the afternoon is like a whole new day. Practice is just as long and grueling. When it's over, those who missed lifting in the morning can do so now. The rest head for dinner and slam down enough food to replenish the calories, vitamins, and electrolytes lost during the afternoon heat. If they don't, they can bet on being twisted into knots by their own cramping muscles later that night. I've seen guys cramp up like that screaming in pain and squirming on the floor like an insect under a magnifying glass. If the body doesn't get enough potassium back, it shuts down.

After dinner the marathon of meetings begins. Special teams is first. During training camp, almost everyone is involved in these meetings. Depth charts are three or four deep, and even if you won't play a down of special teams during the season (which is unlikely) you'll still be on a couple of special teams during training camp. After special teams comes the team meeting where the head coach conducts any administrative business and then proselytizes his particular philosophy on what it takes to win in the NFL. The team then breaks down into offensive and defensive meetings. Film is watched and new plays from the playbook that will be practiced during the next day's sessions are reviewed or added. Next, players break down into meetings with their position coaches once again to watch film of the afternoon practice and go over specific details of the new plays to be installed. If there is any time left, and there usually isn't, position coaches might show game film on an upcoming preseason opponent. The only thing that saves the players from sitting there until well beyond midnight is a coaches' meeting that the head coach usually schedules around nine-thirty or ten. Individual meetings will usually go down to the wire, giving the players only about an hour to socialize, call their wives or girlfriends, or play a game of cards before collapsing in bed in an attempt to be rested for the next day, when the whole process will be repeated again.

The worst aspect of training camp isn't even the drudgery of repeating this schedule day after day for over a month. The worst part is the physical toll it takes on your body and the mental toll it takes on your mind. After just a day or two, injuries compound themselves and waking up in the morning or the middle of the night is not unlike having an incredible hangover, only the aches aren't limited to just your head. Mentally, the deprivation of normal contact with friends and family makes you feel like you're serving a jail sentence. Almost to a man, players wonder aloud why they're doing what they're doing and how many more years they'll continue to do it. The glory and joy of playing in the NFL seem as remote as the moons of Jupiter. Show me a player who doesn't hate football during training camp and I'll show you a lunatic. Never in my life during training camp did I not find myself seriously asking the question: "What the hell am I doing here?"

So the obvious question is, *Why?* Why do teams go through this ritual year after year? Coaches will tell you its purpose is to get the team up to speed and ready to play football at the highest level once the regular season begins. For rookies, maybe this is true. They have to learn a whole new system of football, which can be complex and take a couple of weeks. Most rookies, however, won't be integral starting players for their team anyway. So there is an argument that even they don't *need* to suffer through training camp.

For veterans, camp is not an exercise in enhancing skills they will use during the season, but one of survival. Players don't want to use up their strength, stamina, or health pounding on their teammates. Training camp is nothing but a minefield. Every veteran player in the NFL can hit like a Mike Tyson jab, so there's nothing to prove on that front. And, unless a new coach and a new system has been installed, veterans don't need anything more than a cursory review of the playbook. So, if you consider the detrimental effects training camp can have on veteran players compared to what are only limited advantages at best, the only reason remaining to continue this practice is because it's always been that way. And that is no reason at all.

Veterans get smart though. If their job is safe from serious competition, they'll milk any injuries they might have for all they're worth. There are no feelings of remorse or guilt in doing this either. It's only when a job or a game is on the line that a player will be expected by anyone (outside the coaching staff) to suck up the pain and play on. Another favorite tactic of players is to use the old-fashioned holdout. A holdout can be a marvelous tool. Not only can it alleviate a good hunk of training camp, it can sometimes get you more money. I had three holdouts in my eight-year career, and I was tickled to distraction every day I woke up during the month of August at home, in my own bed.

A short-term solution is to have your wife go into labor during training camp. Guys love nothing more than to get that call in the middle of some hot afternoon practice that their wife is having contractions. It's one of the few things besides a death that can get you out of camp for a couple of days. I do believe that some guys planned their families this way. In fact I know it. Unfortunately for me, my daughter was born a few weeks late. I was already out of camp. The good news was she came on a Wednesday, which is the worst practice of the week during the regular season because of its length and the amount of hitting that goes on.

Some of the more drastic tricks to avoid training camp that I've witnessed were players retiring because of age or injury or quitting because of psychological reasons, and then pulling a move that Sugar Ray Leonard made famous by suddenly changing their minds once the team had broken training camp. Fooled ya. The only problem with that is that your teammates will treat you like a leper. A holdout or milking an injury is socially accepted in the NFL, but not a Sugar Ray retirement. Misery loves company, I guess. If that's true, I promise you no one loves company more than an NFL lug stuck in the mire of training camp.

BRING YOUR PLAYBOOK

The air-conditioner groans and drips as it slowly loses its battle with the August heat. Daylight leaks in from a crevice between the heavy curtain and the window. Otherwise it is dark. The smell of the damp carpet reminds you of a remodeled basement. You lie alone in your room because your roommate is already gone. He didn't make it past the first cut. You remember the shame on his face as he stuffed rumpled T-shirts and plaid boxer shorts into what you know was his father's worn-out plastic suitcase, stuffing them in like groceries, not bothering to fold them. You hopefully suggested that he might get picked up by another team. He might make it yet. But it sounded false to you and you're sure it did to him as well. One good thing, if they come for you, there won't be anyone to lob embarrassing words at you. It will be over and that will be that.

You think about it being over. How long has it been? Fourteen years? You started when you were eight, and since then, whenever people called out your name, "the football player" were always the next words from their mouths, or at least the first thing on their minds. That's what you've been. That's what you are.

There are pictures of you in your college uniform, one knee in the grass and the wind in your hair, at strategic places throughout the universe that makes up your life. Of course your girlfriend has one of these on the dresser next to her bed back at college. There's one in your mom's wallet and another on your father's desk where he works. Your brothers and sisters are represented in a family portrait, but you stand alone in a bright frame gilded with imitation gold. Your grandmother has one on her refrigerator, placed slightly higher than the rest, so that anyone reaching inside for a cold drink or a leftover leg of chicken must first be confronted with the undeniable fact that you are a football player. It seems inconceivable to you that you could be anything but the person portrayed in that picture, the enviable one who's strong and successful and so much in control.

On the other hand, you can sense it coming with the same undeniable foreboding of that pause on the telephone a person will take before they tell you about someone's death. It's not so much what they say to you as what they don't say. The coaches seemed to stop yelling at you several days ago. At first you thought it was because you were getting it right. Then you smartened up and realized it was because they simply stopped caring. Your teammates, or the people you hoped would be your teammates, seemed to have sensed this as well. They don't look you in the eye anymore. You have become an Untouchable among Brahmans. You are unclean and they don't want to touch you for fear the bad luck you obviously have might rub off on them.

Luck has something to do with it too. You know

that now. People think not. People think you either have it or you don't, but it's not true. You have it. Others do too. Sometimes it doesn't matter. You get a bad hand and you lose. There's a rookie linebacker who got lucky. The starter is holding out and the backup got hurt and will be out for the year. During a preseason game, this guy came free on a pass rush and got a sack forcing a fumble that he recovered. He also had a few tackles. If you watch carefully on the film, you can see that the guy blocking him tripped on his own feet. The quarterback didn't see him coming. The ball popped out when he hit him and bounced right into this guy's hands. Talk about luck. The coaches refer to him now as a guy who can make things happen, a big playmaker. You could do the same given the same circumstances, most guys here could. Instead, you lie here waiting.

It is Monday morning. Final cuts must be made by noon tomorrow, but the coaches have told you that things will be taken care of today. That's how they put it, "taken care of." In Saturday night's final preseason game, you secretly prayed for one of the two veterans who play your position to get hurt. You didn't want them to get hurt too badly, not paralyzed, just a knee or hamstring or something. Something that would put them out for the season. Something to give you a chance. Instead, the backup played well and the starter played even better. The only time you saw the field was during the kicking game, but you won't make the team for your talents in that arena.

You're a terrible special teams player. Some people just are. You can't help it, you feel like you're floating in space out there, a battle star whose purpose is to protect the mother planet Earth. Opposing players whiz by you like deadly missiles. You swing and miss and can do nothing but turn and watch their exhaust as they streak downfield toward the runner completely unmolested by you. The impact makes you cringe. The coaches will all watch this play tomorrow ten times over on the game film to assess the talent and effort of their prospective players. You set your jaw and give your fist a shake. Damn! At least they'll know you cared.

You look at the clock. It is almost nine. Despite the knots in your stomach you are hungry, and you think about getting up to go eat. You won't go. You don't want the Turk to get you in the dining hall, where everyone can see you. You'll wait here. Your own suitcase is already packed and in the back of your Bronco. You took care of that last night in the dark. It's a bad feeling to think that the guys who you've lived with for the past month will never really know you're gone. You will disappear from their consciousness like a once-used phone number.

Then hope creeps into your mind. It is unwanted. It is false. You can't help it. It comes. Against your will you imagine that they decide to keep you. They like your effort and they think you will develop. This is not entirely impossible. Stranger things have happened. You've seen guys yourself, ten-year veterans who had stories not unlike your own, late-round draft picks, seemingly dispensable, down on their luck, destined to be cut, but who by some last-minute quirk of fate made it anyway and went on to have meaningful lasting careers. Your pulse quickens. You can envision your girlfriend coming down for a weekend, sitting in the stands on the fifty-yard line with the other wives and girlfriends. You think of the ring you'd buy her with the money from your first paycheck. You can see that check. It would be for about five thousand dollars after taxes, the minimum salary in the NFL, but a fortune to you.

Your parents would come too. It would be a dream come true for them, to sit in the stands of an NFL game and watch their son play. Of course you wouldn't play that much, but you know that if you could just make the team, other opportunities will come. The first year is the hardest. Everyone knows that. Once you've made a roster, you are legitimized in the world of football. Even if you're cut after that, other teams will want you. If you've made it once, you have the indelible mark of approval. There are Pro Bowl players who started out that way. Pro Bowl players make millions of dollars every year. That could be you. Your mind slides easily down this slope of unrealistic optimism. You think about the homes you would own and the cars you would drive. This is interrupted by the sharp knocking at your door.

You jump from the bed and rush to the door. He is standing there looking disheveled and embarrassed. He was up all night with the rest of the coaching staff, making decisions with the gravity of a cadre of generals plotting strategy for the decisive battle in a world war. For the ones who are not worthy, they will send the Turk. He will bring them in and take their playbooks, the battle plan entrusted to each soldier. They will surrender this tome and then be sent away with some false words of encouragement.

The Turk himself is a lowly scout, an ominous bogeyman who is nothing more than a harmless shadow cast by a clump of discarded clothes in the bedroom corner. He doesn't have the majesty of the Grim Reaper. He is simply the lowest man on the totem pole who gets to bring the bad news, a job no one else wants. Still, looking in his beneficent face you think there is hope that they may simply want to tell you that you've made it, that you're one of them, part of the team, welcome aboard.

"Coach wants to see you," he says before delivering the final blow, the words that make your fate undeniable. "Bring your playbook."

JOCKLESS JOCKS

You would think with all the tooth-loosening hits delivered on every play during an NFL game that players would do everything within the realm of science and religion to protect their family jewels. The hard facts are that protective cups, as they're known, are as uncommon in the NFL as painted toenails. Guys just don't wear them.

The first day I suited up in an NFL locker room I was nervous. I didn't know what was going to happen to me out there on the field. Would I survive? I thought yes, but I wanted every possible protection anyway. I had forearm pads and hand pads, elbow pads and thick heavy thigh pads. I had a neck roll, double X shoulder pads, padded gloves, a caged face mask, hip pads, a tailbone pad, a helmet so full with air I looked like a boiled lobster, and, quite sensibly I thought, a cup. In the midst of all this padding I was hard at work when I noticed that some of the guys were staring at me.

"I'm a rookie," I thought. "They're sizing me up. They want to kill me."

"What's that?" a guy next to me finally said, pointing at my crotch.

"What's what?" I said, mystified.

"That?"

"This?" I said, pointing.

"Yes."

"This?" I said, rapping a knuckle against the hard plastic.

"Yes."

"A cup," I said with an embarrassed shrug, wondering if I was the brunt of some enormous joke. "It's a cup. What do you think it is?"

My teammate shrugged and turned away with a shake of his head.

"You don't wear one of those things, do you?" another guy said.

"Yes," I said. "Don't you?"

"No," he told me. "No one wears a cup."

"No one?" I said.

He shook his head and waved his hand up and down the aisle. Beefy chocolate and vanilla thighs were being squeezed into skintight practice pants. Not a cup among them.

Never being one to follow the crowd simply for the sake of conformity, I kept my cup in. I think I kept it for almost a week. But what happened to me, and what happens to most guys who last in the NFL, is that I learned to wear absolutely as little padding on my body as I could possibly bear. The reason is simple: speed. With all that stuff I had on those first few days it's a wonder I could make a single tackle. I was bundled tighter than an Eskimo in a January cold snap. I thought I was pretty safe in all that stuff, but the truth is, if you're about to get run over by a tractor-trailer, your best bet is to sidestep it and get out of the way, rather than being bundled up in pads and trusses and slings that are supposed to help keep you from getting hurt.

There are a few exceptions. Some runners and quarterbacks, who could easily be compared to the ducks in a shooting gallery, will don all the required padding, and then some. Flak jackets, or rib pads, hard shells of plastic covering a couple inches of foam to absorb the shock of a blind-side hit, are pretty standard for quarterbacks. Some runners will cover their bodies with additional armor. Erik Dickerson was the most padded player in the NFL. He had enormous thigh and knee pads, hip pads, rib pads, big linemanlike shoulder pads, and biceps pads. He even had one of those enormous mouthpieces that have a protective outer piece to cover your lips and racquet-ball-like plastic goggles that kept people's fingers out of his eyes. If they'd let him, Dickerson would have worn a medieval suit of armor and I can't say I would have blamed him. With those big guys coming at him full speed from every direction, the only place a runner or quarterback could really be safe on the field would be inside a Volvo.

For the most part though, guys pare down as much as they possibly can. Some guys are even temporarily ejected from the game for not having enough padding. Although that is rare, because the only real requirements are a helmet, some kind of shoulder pads, and any excuse for a knee pad. Thick, half-inch foam knee pads are replaced with thin squares of foam a quarter of that size that amount to nothing more than oversized Band-Aids. Thigh pads are cut up and only the thin plastic filling is extracted and used for protection. Some players' shoulder pads are nothing more than a couple of inches of foam without the typical hard shell on the exterior. Incredible as it may sound, even mouthpieces are optional in the NFL. As I said, no one wears a cup, and many guys have replaced the once ubiquitous jockstrap with nothing more than a pair of cotton shorts.

If you think all this is foolish or crazy, you may be right. But, remember, playing in the NFL is usually a fleeting experience. There is always another willing and able body trying to take your job no matter who you are. There is little players won't do to maximize their performance. If it means taking a little more risk with injuries, or dealing with the pain of some additional bruising, there are very few guys who won't do it. If they don't, they don't last anyway because the biggest difference between college football and NFL football is the speed at which the game is played. You have to move fast and anything that slows you down, or hinders your mobility in the slightest is better left in the locker room, even if it's your jock.

LIFE ON THE INTERSTATE

It is the single most asked question in the life of an NFL player: What's it like? That's understandable. We watch the game on TV, some of us since we were quite young. The entire country watches week after week and then the world for the final contest of the NFL season. It's different than wanting to know what a movie star or a rock star feels like onstage or in front of the camera. It's different because success isn't to be had by simply performing to satisfy the tastes of the audience. Success can only be attained with the physical defeat, the domination if you will, of the opposition, the enemy.

There are many football fans who have experienced the game at the elementary level, in leagues or in high school. The transition from high school football to Division I college football is tremendous. The transition from playing in college to playing in the NFL is overwhelming. Each player was, of course, one of the best from whence he came. Each was a dominant member of the team he played for and had grown accustomed to putting fear or at least concern into the hearts of Saturday afternoon opponents. The NFL is a whole new experience. In one way, it is so different, it's as if you have to learn to play the game all over again. Certain techniques and the use of brute power, things that might have worked against college opponents, are suddenly not as effective.

Almost everyone has had those feelings of disorientation their first day on a new job, or that first time in a new school. You don't know where anything is. You need a map to get around. Most people also know what it feels like to struggle with a skill. It could be ice-skating, waterskiing, windsurfing, or even riding a bike. When you first begin, it seems almost impossible that you could ever be proficient. There are no "naturals;" every person must learn by falling and getting up, time after time. Playing in the NFL takes the emotions inherent in those new undertakings and mixes them in with one new sensation.

The best way to describe the feeling of a player's first moments of an NFL game is to compare it to stepping suddenly out into the middle of a busy interstate. The bodies moving past you and at you are immense, like pickups, sports cars, motorcycles, dump trucks. The speed at which they travel is frightening. You didn't know something with those kinds of mass could move so fast, or if you did, it seems somehow so much more impressive to watch them moving up close. Suddenly you get hit. You reel. You stagger. You try to avoid getting hit again, but once they've got you spinning, you can't recover. It's like one of those dreams where bad guys are chasing you and your feet feel like they're weighted with concrete. Every player's first experience in an NFL game is a deluge of confusion. Anyone who tells you this experience isn't at least initially a little bit frightening is either lying, or just plain crazy.

There's a big difference too when the dust settles.

The feeling on Monday morning is the same feeling I
had one time when I was in a car accident where the
car was totaled. I woke up the next day hurting in
places I didn't know I had. Biological connective tissue,
cushions, levers, hinges, and framing all feel like
they've been shaken at the foundation. Everything feels
a little loose. Everything hurts. The difference between
football and a car accident is that a football game happens every week for twenty weeks in the NFL. A car
accident like that usually only happens once in a lifetime. You suffer through it and go on. But try stringing
twenty of those things together, one a week, and you
find that your body just can't recover. This incredible
pounding is why the rookie season is by far the hardest
for every NFL player. Suddenly college football seems
like nothing more than a series of complicated pillow
fights.

It doesn't last forever, this bewilderment of stepping
out onto the interstate. Like everything else, if you survive, you gradually become accustomed to the size and
the speed and the intensity of the contest. Those big
trucks coming at you don't seem to be moving as fast
as they once did. It's like taking a long trip and setting
the cruise at sixty-five. After a few hours it feels like
you're crawling and you're quite comfortable bumping
it up to eighty. You feel like you can move in and out
of the traffic, not with a great amount of safety, but at
least with a clear head. You flatten some tires of the big
semis as they scream toward or past you. You knock a
few cyclists off their seats. You feel the thrill that makes
it all worthwhile, the thrill of moving down an interstate at mach speed, flirting with disaster.

Things that only a season ago seemed unthinkable
are suddenly second nature and it's almost no big deal
anymore. Your adrenaline flows. You play the game.
You're in the zone. You belong there. The only thing

that never goes away is that haze of insecurity. Because no matter how comfortable and adjusted you become, you're still out there in heavy traffic. You remember what your mother always told you: Don't play in the street. Now you know what she meant. Life on the interstate is always dangerous.

Body Weight:
Can't Live with It,
Can't Live Without It

There are only two types of guys in the NFL, those who are trying to gain weight and those who are trying to lose it. There is no in between. There are The Fats and The Fat-Nots.

This is a particularly sensitive subject with me. I was a Fat-Not. I played my entire eight years in the league trying to gain weight. I was a defensive lineman who struggled on a weekly basis hoping to tilt the scales at two hundred and fifty. Steroids were always an option. I passed. Lots of guys used weight-gain dietary supplements, powders that you could mix into milkshakes that would blast thousands of calories into your system with just one glassful. I simply ate everything that could fit on a plate, and then went back for more.

As you can imagine, this kind of gastronomical behavior would elicit a cacophony of moans and groans every time my wife and I would go out to eat with another couple, especially if the husband happened to be one of The Fats from the team. Inevitably, the dessert cart would come around, and it wasn't a matter of "If?" or "What?" but "How many?" Normal people hate nothing more than a fellow human being who not only *can* eat everything in sight, but one who *has to*. It's disgusting. I know that now myself.

You see, when you play in the NFL, if you have a high metabolism, I will contend that you cannot ingest enough calories to get fat. Your rate of activity is so high that you're a literal calorie-guzzling engine. You have to do everything you can not to lose weight. Once your career is over though, so is the party. That's the revenge everyone else gets. They can watch that same guy who used to complain about having to eat so much, suffer, as he painfully turns down a fat wedge of triple chocolate cake, his favorite.

Of course, Fat-Nots pay a price while they're playing as well, away from the dinner table that is. Ask any of them, Sam Mills, the inside linebacker for the Panthers, Jay Novacek, the tight end for the Cowboys, or Darrell Green, the defensive back for the Redskins. When you're undersized in the NFL, it's like playing rough with your older brother's friends as a kid. When they whump you, you seem to roll a little further, and it seems to hurt you just a little bit more than it does to the bigger kids. Same way in the NFL. I'll never forget having to line up across from the 49ers' triple-extra-large offensive tackle, Bubba Paris. At the time, Bubba outweighed me by at least a hundred pounds. I suspect maybe it was more. Fats always lie about their weight in the program. I was expected to be able to stop that, that three-hundred-fifty-pound load of guts coming at me like a freight train. Not only was I supposed to stop him, I was supposed to toss him aside like a used newspaper. Well, you didn't have to be there to know that it just wasn't going to happen. Simple physics precluded any David and Goliath routine.

Don't laugh, I know what you're thinking. You're thinking about the guy you saw at the A&P on Saturday, the three hundred-plus-pounder with the wagon-load of Twinkies. But you're wrong. Bubba was Fat, true true, but Bubba could beat you to the hoop in basketball. Bubba could race you to the mailbox and win, just so long as it wasn't too far. I'm talking ten or twenty yards. My point is that The Fats in the NFL can move the way most fat people can't. Otherwise they wouldn't be in the NFL.

As a Fat-Not, I relied on quickness to survive. I would go around those big guys, not through them. Bubba, on the other hand, was not only too big to go through, he was too big to get around. Needless to say it made for a couple of long afternoons in the Bay Area before he finally had to retire. I'd go upfield on him, racing for the perimeter of his flank, but inevitably the west wing would collapse on top of me. I must admit that to this day I could do a blindfolded taste test and easily recognize the distinctive taste of the infield of Candlestick Park from, say, the pitcher's mound at Anaheim Stadium. I could put most of those big guys to shame at the beach, but the truth was, when it comes to the battle in the trenches, nothing is quite so useful as a prodigious gut.

But for The Fats in the NFL, life is no big bowl of chocolate-covered cherries either. There is a constant bounty on their bellies. The Fats have weight limits set by their respective coaches. They get fined by the pound, usually fifty to a hundred dollars per, on a weekly basis if they exceed their limit. It's not unusual to see the sauna bulging at the seams on Friday afternoons, the day before official team weigh-ins. Some of The Fats will diet like middle-aged housewives, counting calories and using diuretics in an attempt to keep off the pounds. The rest will indulge themselves during the week, eating steaks and doughnuts like there's no tomorrow, gaining as much as twenty pounds, and stretching their pants two sizes. Then Friday, they'll all wear rubber sweat suits under their pads during practice, hit the bike, then the sauna, and walk around with little paper cups, spitting away those last few ounces just like high school wrestlers. It works too. They can sweat off as much water in a day as you might drink in a month.

Friday night is the real test for the big guys. They know if they go out, each and every drink, and each and every cheeseburger they consume will cost them dearly the next morning. Some of The Fats, the big moneymakers, just say the hell with it. They live the good life and pay hundreds of dollars in weekly fines.

The other liability for The Fats is overtime. One of those big dump trucks may hammer you all day long, but if the game goes into a fifth quarter, they fade like old color photographs. You can leave them huffing in their tracks and jump on the freeway to the quarterback.

Either way, we're all dead when we stop playing. The Fats, because they're finally turned loose like one of those dogs they starve before they shoot an Alpo commercial. The Fat Nots, because they're so accustomed to the see-food diet (see food, and eat it) that they can never really slow down. Their days at muscle beach are numbered. In either case, unless some kind of rigorous daily exercise routine is established, coronary arteries beware. We all blow up like Thanksgiving Day balloons. It's no wonder the life expectancy of an ex-NFL player is rumored to be less than that of a Chernobyl nuclear engineer.

WHAT'S A STINGER?

If you were ever walking down the street and someone hit you and you suddenly got a real stinger, you'd think you were going to die. I used to get stingers in college and in the NFL when they weren't in vogue. Players would get stingers as recently as a few years ago, the same as they do now, only now, suddenly, people around the game of football realize that stingers are dangerous. Surgeries are performed because of stingers. Careers (like Sterling Sharpe's) are ended because of stingers.

In fact I was broadcasting the game for FOX when Sterling Sharpe received that life-altering blow. He was releasing off the line of scrimmage when an Atlanta Falcon safety came running up from the secondary and met Sharpe head-on. Sharpe's head snapped back like a whip and he collapsed on the spot as if shot with a gun. I could see instantly that he'd gotten a stinger. In my zeal for toughness, I predicted that Sterling would go to the sideline, shake it off, and return later in the game. I knew that as a receiver, Sharpe was much less accustomed to such injuries than most linemen are.

That injury, however, would wisely be the end of a superstar career. In short, neurologists are now consulted for these injuries, where before aspirin was dispensed.

A stinger is when the nerves exiting the spinal column through tiny holes in the vertebrae are somehow compressed. This is allegedly caused by several factors. One is that the spinal column itself, or the tiny holes themselves are too small for the bundles of nerves passing through them and therefore the nerves themselves are more sensitive to the shock of an impact. Another is the inflammation of one of the cartilage disks between the vertebrae putting pressure on the outgoing nerves. Finally, there are impacts, or hits, so extraordinary in and of themselves that the nerves in question can be stretched or pinched without any preexisting physical ailment.

When the nerves leaving the trunk of the spine are impinged in this way, the result is excruciating. The only description I can think of is someone plunging a thick rusty dagger into your neck while at that same instant the knife is stuck by a bolt of lightning. The initial pain is a stab, but the ensuing shock travels from your neck upward to your brain and also out to the extremities that the nerve services. In the stingers I've had, the shock normally encompassed the area of the upper right quadrant of my torso. My right arm was rendered temporarily useless, as if I'd woken up after having slept on it wrong. But it wasn't in the numb stage. Rather it was similar to the stage when your arm starts to wake up and there is that tingling sensation of pain and needles. Also short-circuited were my shoulder and chest and my back down to just past the shoulder blade.

The times I had stingers when I wasn't completely incapacitated by an accompanying concussion (which was occasionally the case) I would grit my teeth and swallow the pain hoping that there would be enough time before the next play for the feeling to return to my arm and the pain to subside enough so that the tears would stop streaming down my face. When I think of a stinger, the image of tears is the first thing that comes to mind. I can see myself staggering in place in the defensive huddle, trying to keep from toppling over like a tower of poorly stacked blocks, with tears streaming uncontrollably down my face from the pain. I would emit a primal growl of anger in defiance of the pain that was threatening to force me to my knees.

An incident like a bad stinger is so intense that afterward you would wonder if the whole thing wasn't imagined. After all, how could something be so painful and yet allow you to live? But a stinger leaves a distinct calling card to let you know that you've been struck. In the safety of the locker room, after the game, when I would peel off my sweat-sodden gear, I would be reminded of the nerve damage by the peculiar hypersensitivity of the skin in the affected area. Even a gently placed finger on my chest, back, neck, or arm would somehow complete a little electrical circuit sending off small lights and buzzers in my brain. In that state, a postgame shower became an agonizing experience. I was told that this sensitivity was simply a residual of the nerve trauma.

Unfortunately, once you have a stinger, the likelihood of irritating that nerve again is greatly increased. Once the nerve is injured, like any other part of the body there is swelling in the immediate area. That swelling only serves to constrict the already small space that the nerve has to travel through the complex structures of the neck. It was not unusual for me to get a stinger early in a game and then get four or five more before the afternoon was over. The most difficult part about this was continuing to throw my body in front of running backs and to continue to smash head-on with three-hundred-pound linemen who were coming at me off the line as quick as the kick of a horse. Looking back, it's one of those things that will make me thankful if my boys decide not to play the game at all.

Because the functioning of the nervous system is so difficult to calibrate, and because pain itself is impossible to measure, stingers remain nebulous injuries. During the eight years of my career, however, I watched as stingers were taken more and more seriously. Where before the term "stinger" or "pinched nerve" was used to generically assume that if the player was tough enough, he could simply grit his teeth and go on, now these injuries are examined with much more gravity. MRIs, X-rays, and neurological evaluations are common practice after a player gets a stinger. Players are advised or choose to retire because of stingers that before were simply tolerated with great discomfort and possibly with danger.

I think as time goes on, stingers will be taken more and more seriously. The old-time players will gripe and moan that the football players of tomorrow just aren't what they used to be, and they'll be right. I have the feeling that the players of the future will be much smarter.

How to Shake Hands
with an NFL Player

If you've ever met an NFL player you've shaken hands with him. I hope you did it right. It's not difficult to learn, but you don't want to screw it up, or the player you've just met will walk away thinking you are a consummate buffoon.

The world is full of men (and women) who think that initial impressions are everything. They think that it is critical upon meeting someone new that they give every indication that they are strong and successful and not to be taken lightly. They think that the best way to do this is to put your hand into a crushing vise grip. They usually catch the rest of us off guard, because we are simply shaking hands as a courtesy, not to establish our dominance like some dog lifting his leg on a post.

I met people like this everywhere I went as an NFL player. Because I was a member of the NFL, an occupation known for its requisite of physical prowess, these bad-handers would get an extra flow of adrenaline when they saw my hand outstretched in naive greeting. They hurt me. Time and time again with their manly

44

clasps they would leave me reeling in my shoes, fighting with all my will not to curse them out on the spot.

The reason is simple. When you play in the NFL, especially if you play on the line, your hands are like pouches of corned beef hash. Under the skin (if in fact the skin itself isn't broken with numerous cuts) everything else feels like it's been ground up. Imagine the worst hangover or headache that you've ever had. Now imagine that same ache in your hands. Now you're there. The joints on almost every digit are swollen by September. Many players don't wear their wedding rings during the season. My own ring was guaranteed to be stuck below the inflamed lower knuckle of my ring finger until at least February when the swelling could finally have a chance to subside. During practices and games, players have to bear the implicit pain from having bruised and swollen hands. What they don't have to put up with is shaking hands with fools.

So when you meet a big tough NFL player, realize that the bigger and tougher he is, the more likely his hands will be as delicate as a butterfly's wings. Instead of showing him how tough you are, show him how smart you are. Shake his hand as gently as possible without resembling a soggy noodle. When he tells you it was nice to have met you, he'll be telling the truth, instead of cursing you under his breath as you walk away.

Racism in the NFL

You would think that the world of NFL football would be the ideal setting for blacks and whites to interact free from racial biases or tensions. You might even think that they do, but you would be wrong. This is despite the fact that most football players in the NFL come from the same backgrounds: middle- to lower-income families, four or five years of college experience, newfound wealth, young, and suddenly alone in a new city to which they have been drafted.

Whenever a team travels anywhere, two large buses are needed to move them. It is not uncommon for one bus to be predominantly filled with blacks and the other with whites. This self-imposed segregation is also evident in where the different groups of players sit on the airplane, the makeup of players in a card game, who rooms with whom on the road, and who sits with whom at the dinner table. This voluntary segregation is so obvious that I'm sure it wouldn't surprise the casual observer to see signs reading, THIS TABLE, BLACKS ONLY or WHITE PLAYERS TO THE BACK OF THE PLANE. It's already as if the signs are there and most players are obeying them.

Why? you might ask. It's simple. The hard facts are that black and white players on a whole talk differently, walk differently, listen to different music, drive different cars, and even dress differently. And, just like everywhere else in society, these differences breed mistrust. I'm not saying that there aren't white players who drive gold-rimmed Mercedes or black ones who don't drive Ford F-350s with dual rear wheels. Mercifully, there are guys who do mix in the NFL, black guys who love to go deer hunting with their backwoods white counterparts, and white guys who tap their feet and blow out the bass in their speakers to the hard-core rap of Snoop Doggy Dogg. There are whites who sit at the predominantly black dinner tables and blacks who ride on the predominantly white buses, but the tendencies are undeniable. There are coaches in the NFL who attempt to break these tendencies down. Some require roommates in training camp and on the road to be interracial. This is a good thing, but only if the players are receptive to it. If they're receptive, they can learn that their differences are outward only and actually come to appreciate them. However, if they're not receptive, forcing interracial players to live together only breeds further contempt and mistrust.

From the perspective of an unenlightened white player, blacks who drive extravagant cars and wear extravagant clothes and jewelry are simply flaunting their newfound wealth. The rap music played in the locker rooms and on the buses and planes is loud and offensive to them. Some whisper racial epithets among themselves, cursing the blacks for their "ghetto" ways.

One black player, and a good friend of mine, explained the show of money this way:

"If I walk into a store at the mall wearing a pair of

ragged jeans and a T-shirt, the people in the store will follow me around like I'm going to steal something. I *have* to dress nice and wear an expensive watch for most people to simply assume I'm not a criminal. That doesn't happen to you because you're white."

This same player has felt on more than one occasion the humiliation of going to rent an apartment that was advertised in the paper and having the landlord say that it was no longer for rent. In fact, it seems most black players, like most black Americans, have had similar experiences.

If you ask black NFL players about the league they're in, almost to a man, you will find that they believe without a doubt that the racism they see throughout society is mirrored exactly in the NFL. Although for years blacks have made up a substantial majority of the players in the league, the number of black coaches and front office people remains grossly disproportionate. Black players see this and believe that it is intentional. Of course the prerequisite for coaching and managing a football team is experience in and around the game, so, with most of the people in and around the game being black, their argument certainly makes sense.

"It starts at the top," one black player told me. "You've got white owners who hire white people for the front office who hire white head coaches who in turn hire white assistant coaches. Except for an occasional token black, the system is dominated by whites, and as long as the owners are all white, it will always be that way."

Recently, I had a discussion about the subject of black team ownership with Jesse Jackson and *USA Today* writer Bryan Burwell. They disagreed with the notion I had adopted from my black teammates that indeed there should be black ownership in the NFL.

Bryan Burwell suggested that this would only create a bastion of black coaches and front office personnel and would do nothing to further the cause of integrated equality. Jesse Jackson complained that players in the NFL have the power to demand more black coaches and front office people and suggested that black NFL players were wimps for not creating an uproar over the issue.

I disagree with Bryan Burwell. I think black ownership would, if nothing else, have great symbolic importance to black players in the NFL. Jesse Jackson is just flat wrong. Yes, black players do have the power to demand more representation on the coaching staffs and in the front offices. But the very nature of a football player, and one of the essential elements to ever get to the NFL, is to maintain ranks. As a football player, it is ingrained in your mind from childhood that you listen to your coaches and toe the line. Those who don't, never make it past the high school JV squad. Football is a game that requires the discipline and unquestioning obedience of a soldier. Right or wrong, the fact is that all football players are programmed to march to a certain beat. To expect black players to rise up and begin making demands of the NFL, shucking the mentality that got them to the big leagues in the first place, is unrealistic without the existence of a strong and vocal leader among their ranks.

I believe that race relations between whites and blacks are better in the NFL than almost anywhere else in our society. But still, if racism exists here, then how far off the mark are we? Because blacks and whites have the unusual opportunity in the NFL to find themselves on equal footing with similar backgrounds, it is important that they learn to eradicate racial bias and show the way for the rest of society. There is no great racial majority here. The responsibilities of ending racism in the NFL fall to two parties.

First, NFL owners should make it their business to earmark one of their next expansion franchises to a minority millionaire. They're out there. I agree with most of the African-American players I spoke with: It starts at the top. Second, the players themselves, black and white, must make individual and concerted efforts to break down their self-imposed codes of segregation. I'm not saying one should adopt the codes of behavior or dress of the other, just be around it, and tolerate it. If they did, I contend that more and more whites would find they like to eat soul food and more and more blacks would find they like country-western music. If nothing else, the exposure to different things would take the fear out of the unknown. NFL players and owners alike need to lead the way, spreading the message that there is only one race, the human race.

DEION SANDERS:
THE MAN, THE MYTH,
THE LEGEND

A lot of readers will turn to this chapter before any other. Some people won't even buy the book. They'll just stand in the bookstore and read about Deion, then go home. Maybe that's what you're doing right now. Deion would love it. You'd be playing right into his hands. Because if you're like so many other people I know, whether you loathe or idolize Deion Sanders, he fascinates you.

There are essentially two Deions. The one most people see, and the one some revile, would be heralded as a marketing genius had he come from the upper crust, attended Harvard for four years, then gone on to get his MBA from Wharton. Deion did no such things. Nonetheless, he has done more on his own, with his instinct for drama and his exceptional athletic ability, than any Madison Avenue marketing machine could have with a staff of fifty. He deliberately and single-handedly created his own kind of celebrity, something very different from anything America has seen before, much less the NFL. He's flashy and loud, drawing people's attention like a Super Bowl commercial. At the same time, he's mysteriously admired and adored by those who know him.

The other Deion is there for those who care to take a closer look, for those who will take the time to simply wait until showtime is over and the actors remove their masks. If, of course, you have a pass to get backstage. Yet, even then, when the lights are down and the makeup and the costumes and the affectations have been set aside, Deion can confuse. He is a complex man. Humble, yet tremendously confident and viciously proud. Clever, but kind. A team player, one of the boys, but almost secretive in his privacy. Comfortable with the hardened dialect of the streets, yet nearly puritanical in his mode of day-to-day living.

When Deion came out of college from Florida State, he did so with the flash of a pie tin spinning in the wind on a hot summer day. Like it or not, if you followed sports, you had to notice Deion. At first, he got his foothold in the minds of American sports fans with his brash talk and his piles of outrageously garish jewelry. He talked a talk that few people figured he could ever walk, and most wrote him off as simply the next Brian Bosworth or Tony Mandarich, college players who tripped and stumbled on their own untamed tongues once they finally got to the NFL. But for Deion, the initial flash was only the beginning, like a child's Roman candle, set off prematurely before the full-blown Fourth of July fireworks really begin.

The first real report was heard literally the moment Deion laid hands on an NFL football in Fulton County Stadium in Atlanta. After touching off an incredible display of speed and moves Deion dashed into the end zone. That ability is what separates Deion as a personality from so many of the others who dare to stand up and make us notice them. Deion has speed. He's the fastest man in the world. Ever. Carl Lewis? Ben Johnson?

Wrong. Deion Sanders has taken the human race to a new top speed. All you have to do is see him to know. I've been on the same field when he's intercepted a pass and taken it back for a touchdown. I've seen him up close as he tears up the field, faster than the rest, and then, if someone has a chance to cut him off at the pass, Deion has a turbo rocket that kicks in and leaves you wondering if you saw what you really saw. It's a beautiful thing.

After his brilliant beginnings in the NFL, Deion spent his off-season with the New York Yankees' Triple A farm team trying to learn how to hit a baseball in the big leagues. People guffawed and pointed their fingers. They snickered at him out loud. They said he was a Bo Jackson wannabe. He never wavered. He simply bought a batting cage and had it installed in his backyard. In 1992, the sports world's jaw hit the floor when he batted .533 in the World Series. He'd fly helicopters from Falcons football practices in Suwanee, Georgia, to the Braves' stadium downtown. That way he could be ready for Sunday's contests in the NFL and still be there for the first pitch in the Series games during the week. One weekend during that same time he took a late-night flight on a private jet from Pittsburgh where the Braves were playing the Pirates to Miami where the Falcons were to play the Dolphins the very next morning. Only the media complained about that incident, the guys upstairs in the booth. The players, from both sports, applauded his determination and his ability to do both.

Deion has always had something that no other NFL player had: an option to walk away. While the rest of us slaved and groveled for jobs with teams whether we wanted to be there or not, Deion was busy telling ownership from both worlds that he could live with them or without them. It is an enviable position to be in, and believe me, a lot of NFL players live vicariously through Deion Sanders. It's because he doesn't need the NFL. Unlike Michael Jordan, Wayne Gretzky, or Greg Norman, he can walk away from his primary sport and not only still make millions of dollars, but still satisfy that need to be a sports hero, something that drove Jordan back to basketball.

But maybe I'm not telling you anything you don't know. It's not hard to see that Deion Sanders is a rare athlete, even if some people have a hard time admitting that fact. And, if you can't see it, you've probably heard Deion himself talking about his unusual talents. Some people say that's bad. I say this is a man who has learned to give the media and the public what they want. Certain people like to grumble that the athletes of today just aren't what they were. I disagree. This is only more grumping from old-timers wishing they were young again. I think rather than athletes not being what they were, that it is the focus of the media that has changed. Now the stories we see and read are about the players who can make the most outrageous noise, rather than the ones who are necessarily the best at what they do or the kind of player who reminds us of the boy next door. Deion learned from Muhammad Ali that America can't resist a bigmouth athlete who can really back up what he says in the arena. He knew that a financial empire could be built from endorsement money for a talented player with the ability to put on a little show every time a camera or microphone was within striking distance.

So, am I saying that the Deion Sanders you see and hear is not necessarily the real Deion Sanders? Yes, that's what I'm saying. He's playing a part, and he's played it so well to date that even at the commonly nondescript position of cornerback, he has made himself into a nationally recognized celebrity. He played it so well he got Dallas Cowboys owner Jerry Jones to give him thirteen million dollars just to sign his name. Now the two of them star in commercials together.

So who is Deion? Just a good guy, not unlike most of the guys you find throughout the world of the NFL. A good friend, a good family man, a good teammate, and believe it or not, an excellent role model for kids. Why? Simple. Just go right down the list: Late nights? No. Bad language? No. Drugs? Never. Alcohol? No. Hardworking? Yes. Smart? Yes. Loyal friend? Always. Devoted father? Better believe it.

If you were a friend of mine and I'd taken you to the Falcons locker room after a practice, you'd have met a lot of nice guys, regular guys. Deion, however, would have stood out in your mind as he did with so many of my other friends. In the midst of all the hustle and bustle, he'd take the time to ask my brother, or my college roommate, or whomever, how they liked Atlanta or where they were from. More than anyone else, he'd make people feel like they belonged there, in the middle of all those hulking and hurrying half-naked bodies, clad in towels, trying to get out of the locker room and head for home.

Gary Plummer, the 49ers' inside linebacker, got to find out what I'm talking about firsthand when Deion joined San Francisco in the 1994 season. He didn't like the notion of Deion coming to San Francisco. Plummer's not a flashy guy and he never appreciated his fellow athletes who were. Deion, he hated. One day, he told me, only he and Deion remained at the facility. It was late and they were the last two to leave for the day. Plummer grudgingly found himself in a conversation with a guy who was nothing like what he had appeared to be from a distance. Their talk turned to baseball, something Plummer could relate to since his young son at the time thought and talked of nothing else. Without a request, without a word about it, Plummer found on his locker stool the next morning a brand-new major-leaguer's glove with Deion's autograph on it for his son.

When Deion scored that first NFL touchdown the first time he touched the ball in Atlanta, he celebrated, yes, as he always does when he scores. Hey, it adds color to the game. If you don't like it, go to a chess match. What you won't see the man do is taunt his fellow player. The very day after his spectacular debut Deion also took the time to go out to the mall and buy every other member of that kick return team a Gucci wristwatch. He didn't do it for the publicity or to make friends. There was no fuss, no muss. He just left the watches sitting on those guys' locker stools for them to find the next day when they arrived for practice. He did it to thank the guys he said he couldn't have done it without. That humility and his relentless pursuit of excellence on the playing field, be it practice or game day, is why anyone who's played with Deion is proud to have called him a teammate. Even the most red-necked country boys in the NFL have to admit that Deion is an asset as well as a pleasure to have on your team.

When it comes to race, Deion fulfills common stereotypes. He's got the walk, the talk, the music (he makes his own rap), the clothes, the dialect, the numerous flashy black cars, the pounds of gold jewelry. At the same time, you couldn't find a guy more unbiased. In my chapter on racism I said that NFL players need to integrate at the individual level. Deion's one of the ones already doing it. You're just as apt to see him in a discussion or a card game with a white guy as a black guy. He was constantly organizing fishing trips for the guys in Atlanta. Guys from every corner of the country would go with him. Guys with skin color as varied as a color bar. The only thing Deion wanted to know was whether or not you liked to fish, never mind whether or not you looked the part. When Nike shot Deion's "Sanderclaus" Christmas promotional ad for TV in 1992, they told Deion he'd need to find three brothers to act as his elves in the spot. Deion told them that was fine, but he'd also be bringing some of his white brothers as well.

The only players I ever saw who didn't like Deion were the ones who were trying to beat him at his own game, the publicity-hungry few who would do anything to keep the cameras on themselves and away from the others around them. Deion is so good at attracting the press now that he doesn't even have to try, and believe me, there are others out there who lie awake in bed at night figuring and scheming to get the cameras off their teammates and on themselves. For all his manipulation of the media, I never once saw Deion begrudge the attention or honors given to another guy. I saw him squeeze owners for every last dime, then turn around and have the audacity to take that walk upstairs and tell management that they should cough up more money for someone else.

When you watch the man play football this fall, you might have a hard time believing all I'm telling you. Sometimes Deion does and says things that make me wonder if it's me that's not just crazy. But then I'll see him somewhere, or talk to him on the phone, and I realize it's just the two faces of Deion, fooling me again. Because behind the myth and the legend, there is a man anyone would like to bring home to dinner.

Painful Days and Sleepless Nights: Prescription Drugs in the NFL

Whenever I had an injury as a player in the NFL, I'd dig into my black bag for some medicinal relief. Over my eight years in the league, I built up an impressive supply of prescription drugs I'd gotten from the team doctor. You get hurt all the time in the NFL, and they'll gladly give you little pills to get you back onto the field quicker. Inevitably, you end up with a little left over here, a little left over there, and what can I say? I was never a guy to flush his unused prescription drugs down the drain. Those little babies came in quite handy.

More than anything, Motrin was my drug of choice. It's an all-purpose anti-inflammatory that can ease the pain of a freshly torn up knee or an old broken bone. If an elbow or a knee was ever throbbing the night before a game, then it was time to drop a hammer, that's Halcion for you neophytes. One little chip of that stuff and you're out like a light. I had plenty left over from a horrible bout of insomnia I had during training camp one time and, like everyone else around me, I didn't hesitate to use it to get some rest the night before a big

58

game. If I ever had a headache that just wouldn't quit? Nothing ever said goodbye to that like a little Tylenol with codeine I had left over from the time I broke my elbow.

When I read my own words, I'm taken aback. I feel like a character from *Drugstore Cowboy*. There was a time, back before I played in the NFL, when I was a purist. I was one of those people who didn't even like to take aspirin. Oh, I always maintained certain limits, but I also came to understand how the lines can fade, and how some guys ended up going way overboard. Every player knows he makes ten times more than his parents ever dreamed of, and he feels an obligation to go out there on Sunday and earn it. The problem is in drawing the line between preparing to play and actual performance enhancement.

I think what happens is this: First a guy will drink coffee to stay alert during a game. Next, he'll take caffeine pills or Up Time for a little something extra. Before you know it, he's showing you a little bottle from some friend that's filled with full-blown amphetamines. Then there's anti-inflammatories. First it's Advil, then Motrin, next it's Indocin, and finally a guy goes on Butazolidin where he has to get blood work every couple of weeks to make sure he isn't killing off all his blood cells. It's the same with muscle-builders. First it's some harmless protein supplement, then steroids, then Clenbuterol, the drug of choice for race horses, and finally, human growth hormones.

To me, all that stuff is way over the line, but even doctor-prescribed drugs and coffee were over the line when I started out. Now I think the moderate use of some drugs is just a necessary reality of big-time football. I expanded my boundaries, but nowhere near the point of abuse. But looking back to my youth, the days when I boasted to the other guys in the neighborhood that when I made it, I'd never have anything in my system stronger than orange juice, I can't help but admit that I have been slightly corrupted.

THOUGHTS FROM INSIDE AN MRI

A magnetic resonance imaging machine is a big fat tube with a small hole through the middle of it. You get strapped to a table that protrudes from that hole like some mechanical tongue. The tongue slowly retracts and you're crammed into the machine. For a guy as big as me it's like stuffing a sleeping bag into the dryer. So there I was with only two inches between my nose and the top wall and my arms pinned to my sides. I began to think. How did I get there? I'd hyperextended my elbow in the game against the New England Patriots, stretching ligaments, tearing muscle fiber, and even cracking a bone, but the answer went beyond that.

My parents told me when I was a boy that if I was going to play the game of football I had to expect to get hurt. How do you expect to get hurt though? You can't. You almost have to pretend it can't happen to you, like it's some bizarre murder you read about that happened in some small town you've never heard of. "That stuff would never happen here," you say. Because if you really stopped and thought about it, about how you were

61

going to get hurt, you might decide it just wasn't worth it. I bet that's what happened to Al Toon, the wide receiver for the Jets who retired a few years ago after suffering his ninth concussion. I bet Al woke up one morning and said enough is enough. Once you say that, once you start thinking about the imminence of getting hurt, you just have to call it quits.

The time in the tube went slowly. The machine pounded loudly as it extracted images of my elbow for doctors to examine. I wanted to move, to stretch, and run. But I was okay. I knew when they were done, they would just push some buttons and I would slide out and walk away.

The nightmare of every football player is what happened to Dennis Byrd in New York and Mike Utley in Detroit, being paralyzed from a broken neck. That's the real scary thing about the profession, the idea that what happened to them could happen to anyone. Doctors who studied the film of Dennis Byrd's injury said if he'd kept his head up he wouldn't have broken his neck. But that's just not something you think about when you're on the field. Every player knows he's not supposed to tackle with his head down, but every player also knows that sometimes it just happens in the barely controlled mayhem on the field. It's like roulette, sooner or later, the ball's gonna drop on someone's number.

When you think of Dennis Byrd or Mike Utley, getting hurt the way I did was no big deal. I knew I would heal. I knew that before my career was over I would run and tackle and dive and hit again, and do all the things that made me feel so alive while I was playing the game. But when I got back from that injury you can be sure I planned on never getting hurt again. And something like Mike Utley? That was too dark, too awful . . . I'm sorry, I couldn't even think about it.

BAD MEN

Despite the common stereotype of the hulking dumb jock who's just as likely to rape, pillage, and kill as an eighth-century Viking, most football players are the kind of guys you wouldn't mind if your daughter married. I'm not just saying that to make my father-in-law happy, even though in truth he did tell my wife when he first heard of our relationship to steer clear from any guy who played the game of football. I can't defend all the guys who put on the pads either. Some are as bad as the hardest criminals in the highest maximum-security prisons across the land. The reality of the situation is that football players are just like almost any other cross section of our society. They're not particularly dumb, or particularly mean. They're not particularly smart or angelic for that matter. They're just average Joes.

Well, not completely average. Let's face it. You have to have a certain recessive gene that has a little something to do with the brain to go out on the football field and beat your head against other human beings on a daily basis. I will grant you that that is not entirely normal. But let's go beyond the obvious one small intellectual deficiency, which doesn't necessarily preclude all other forms of intelligence. There are football players who have gone on to become doctors, lawyers, Supreme Court justices, concert pianists, sculptors, scientists, college professors, and business tycoons.

All right, these fellows are the exceptions, but so are the ones who end up in jail. The press, however, only tells us about the extremes, and more likely than not, only the negative extremes at that. But this is what we, the American public, want. We want to have our generalizations confirmed. It's comforting to think that everything is in order, that priests and doctors are benevolent and good, that politicians and lawyers are corrupt, and that football players are bad men. Also, we don't want to read about people who haven't done anything particularly spectacular. Our society is like the parent who only notices the kid when he shoots out the neighbor's windows with a BB gun, or gets failing grades on his report card.

Our ears perk up when we hear about an athlete who got into a bar fight, discharged a firearm, got busted for drugs, wrecked his car, killed himself, went bankrupt, or beat up his wife. We'll listen to the radio, watch the TV, or pick up the paper for that kind of news. And so, we cast our vote for more of it, telling sponsors to put their dollars down on the news that shocks and horrifies. That's why you don't read about most guys in the NFL. The average guys. No one wants to know about the nose guard who got up the night before to feed the baby at 3 A.M., or the wide receiver who took his day off to go fishing with his daughter. We all do that. It's no big deal, and neither are the lives of most NFL players. They're fathers and husbands, going to work in the morning, doing a job, and coming home with a paycheck.

People mistake the violence of the sport for the violence of the men. The difference between an NFL player and the average guy on the street is not that the player is more likely to break someone's nose. The NFL player has simply learned how to tap into the dark side of the human psyche. We all have it, that dark side. Most football players can turn that on and off like a blender. You need to be bad on the playing field, vicious and mean, that's part of the game. That is the game.

There are, though, some who cannot separate the violence of the game from real life. They have tapped into the dark side but have no shutoff valve. We call them criminals. They mistake life for an extension of the playing field where you hit hard and you hit first, where bashing someone unconscious is a badge of honor and breaking bones is a treat. These guys are why the NFL has a no-firearm policy for players during training camp. The league knows that some of these guys might take the battle on the practice field into the hotel corridors and they don't want anyone getting capped as early in the season as August.

The scariest guy I ever met in the NFL was Charles "Too Mean" Martin. He's the only guy in the unruly history of football ever to be cut from a team because he was too mean. After being released from the Green Bay Packers where he was disciplined for having a bounty list of the numbers of opposing players he wanted to knock out of the game, and a brutal late hit where he hip-tossed Bears quarterback Jim McMahon, separating his shoulder, he was picked up by the Atlanta Falcons. Charles never did anything to me or anyone on the team that would justify calling him a criminal, but he scared the hell out of me all the same. He had that faraway look in his eyes that made you wonder if he was going to say hello, or knock your block off. He was the kind of guy who could walk into a room and give you a chill down your spine.

Still, you can rest assured that the vast majority of the men you see on the NFL fields on Sunday afternoons are pretty tame off the gridiron. They're the guys who talk to your kids at schools throughout the country warning them against the perils of drugs and trying to give them role models to look up to. They're the ones who donate money and time to homeless shelters in their areas, who visit children's hospitals, who open doors for old ladies walking into the mall. They're the kid next door, the one who cut your lawn in the summer and shoveled your driveway in the winter. They're the ones who worked a little harder and sacrificed a little more to grab that gold ring of life in the NFL, but deep down, they're just like you and me.

ALCOHOL AND THE NFL

Sure football players go together with beer like wine goes with cheese. Show me an NFL team on a Friday night and I'll show you ten empty kegs of beer. Only a few players who go through the NFL are bereft of stories about drunken nights filled with bleary-eyed camaraderie. The one thing you won't find though is players playing the game drunk. Unlike baseball where you hear stories all the time of players being so inebriated from the night before that they're still drunk during the ball game, football players have to be stone sober to play or risk being killed.

The NFL itself has tried to distance its players from beer drinking somewhat, although certainly they aren't ready to stop making a buck from selling suds or advertising it. But the NFL does not allow beer in locker rooms or clubhouses, unlike major league baseball. Some teams have even gone so far on their own as to ban beer from their charter flights home. I watched this evolution firsthand and I know that preventing football players from drinking is as realistic as Prohibition in the 1920s. You can make all the rules and policies that you want, but football players are going to drink and drink hard.

When I first got to the Falcons in 1986, there was no limit to the amount of beer you could consume on the team plane. Home games were the same formula where the team would gather at whatever establishment about town was offering free food and drinks to induce the players and coaches to come. Coaches and players alike would hoist the cold cans in either celebration of victory or commiseration of failure.

The ride home on the highway going north from the airport on any given Sunday night in Atlanta when the team traveled was an adventure. Foreign sports cars would pass you like comets if you were poking along at say seventy or seventy-five miles an hour. It took a few DUIs and some guys ramming through the barricades at the airport parking toll booths for the team to ultimately limit the amount of beer to three cans per guy. Of course then everyone became the best friends of the few teetotalers who could cash their three cans in for an unlimited supply of back slaps and toasts to their health. Other guys reverted to their days as kids at sleepaway camp, plotting and scheming how to grab more than their limit of three cans before boarding the plane.

Then when Jerry Glanville signed on as head coach, he eliminated the beer on Falcon charter flights altogether. It didn't matter though. You can no sooner separate an NFL team from their alcohol than you can a baby from its bottle or a cop from his gun. The guys simply got imaginative. Duffel bags turned into coolers and shaving kits into liquor cabinets. Orange juice, club soda, ice, and wedges of lime were still provided by the team.

Unbelievably, the only other time players drink as much as after a game is during training camp. As bad as camp is, as sore and as tired as everyone feels, many players still find it in themselves to sneak away from camp even if it's only for a half hour and get themselves slightly intoxicated. I think the reason for this is because the day is so hard and so intense, that guys need to come down fast. A cold beer is like pulling the emergency brake on a runaway train. And after sweating the entire day out on a field in the summer heat, the body is almost totally dehydrated. Under those circumstances, when you take that first drink, I swear you can feel even that little bit of alcohol travel from your stomach, through your blood, and right to your brain. After about two beers, it's hard for even the big guys to keep from slurring their words. Many times after an afternoon practice has ended a substantial part of the team will hurry down the street to the nearest bar, get drunk, and then return before dinner even begins.

The only one unbreakable rule regarding alcohol is that you can't safely walk onto a football field drunk. Things happen too fast in the NFL, and like a boxer, the opponent is trying to do more than score points. He's trying to hurt you. When someone is swinging his forearm at your head or throwing his body at your knees, you can't afford to be slowed down by alcohol. Hungover you can be, as long as the vast amount of alcohol is out of your system. A painful headache for some guys is like a thorn in a lion's paw. It just makes them madder and more dangerous on the field. Some guys I knew actually swore they played their best games with the most evil hangovers tormenting them. They were that mean.

I don't know why it is football players drink so much. Maybe it's just because it's one more way to preserve the irresponsibility of life's adolescence, that never having to really quite grow up. In that way as well as some others, the whole NFL experience is like an endless fraternity party. Since I left the game I've found that I don't drink much at all, although the habit of getting together with the guys every once in a while and tossing a few down will probably never die completely. Still, looking back, I can see how someone who didn't know about the prevalence and social acceptance of drinking in the NFL could have thought I had a drinking problem that I couldn't control. I didn't and I don't. However, the sad fact remains that while all the laughing and toasting and celebrating is going on, some football players are learning how to destroy themselves and their families in the name of old-fashioned camaraderie and a good time.

GROUPIES: SEX, SEX, AND MORE SEX?

Most of you who at one point or another fantasized about being big-time professional football players out on the prowl will be happy to know that it never guaranteed anyone women falling at his feet. In short, you probably didn't miss a thing. The fact is that, despite their gold Rolex watches and brand-new candy apple red Porsches, NFL players are as likely to strike out on a Friday night as the computer nerd from your Physics 401 class in college.

Sure NFL players score. Who doesn't, eventually? But don't think for a minute that the stories about groupies throwing themselves on guys in nightclubs or in the parking lot after games happens as a matter of course. On the other hand, don't mistake guys like Joe Montana for the average football player either. Joe would see a hot-looking model in a magazine on a plane ride from San Francisco to wherever and when he touched down he'd get his agent on the phone and tell him to find her and fly her in. That was Joe. But he was more than just an NFL player. Joe was a celebrity. You know, like a Tom Cruise type of guy. Most play-

ers, no matter how good-looking they are, no matter
how much money they have, or how many nice cars
they drive, still have to work pretty hard to meet
women.

The problem is that of the two types of women in the
world, groupies and nongroupies, any player possessing
all his senses would wildly prefer a nongroupie. Real
groupies present all sorts of dangers. First, a real groupie
will travel around between guys and even different
sports teams, bringing with her various sorts of abom-
inable "luggage," or diseases, which she is more than
happy to share. Second, for the married scoundrels, a
groupie is like a live hand grenade without the pin. She
is usually short on self-respect, discretion, and tact. In
other words, she's more apt than not to show up at the
doorstep or call the house, wife or no. Flying saucepans,
broken dishes, and divorce usually ensue. Third, there
exists a virulent form of groupie whose main objective in
life is to become impregnated by a plethora of professional athletes, have numerous bastards, and live comfortably off of the various child support payments she
receives. Once caught in her trap, the player can never
escape.

Nongroupies, on the other hand, have usually been
forewarned that football players are one step removed
from a lower form of reptile. They have the fervent belief, as do many people, that NFL players have spent
the past year sleeping with three hundred and sixty-five
different groupies. They want nothing to do with them.
So, NFL players out there, hustling on Friday nights,
trying to score, are actually at a distinct disadvantage
to the rest of the sensitive, unassuming male popula-
tion. Don't you feel better now?

WHAT ABOUT AIDS?

People don't think much about AIDS when they think of NFL football. Oh, maybe certain promiscuous lifestyles create a risk of AIDS among some players, although the players themselves to date haven't been concerned enough to change their lifestyles. One former NFL player, Jerry Smith, a tight end for the Redskins, even died of AIDS. But people disregarded this because he was gay. The league itself has reviewed and considered the possibility of transmission of the virus on the gridiron and dismissed it as inconceivable.

The odds of such a transmission are admittedly very remote. Even transmission of the AIDS virus in medical surroundings where people have had open wounds or the mucus membrane of the eye comes into direct contact with infected blood is unusual, about one of two hundred people thus exposed ever contracts the virus. However, if you're the one, the sentence is death. Football players themselves are not thrilled with the idea of even these remote odds.

I'll never forget the first time I was really dosed with blood after this issue came to the forefront of the news.

We were playing the Redskins at RFK Stadium. It was the same week Magic Johnson brought the whole AIDS issue to the attention of the sports world. I walked off the field at the end of the game and saw that my pants at the thigh had been soaked with blood. I hurried to the locker room and tore off my uniform. The thermal underwear underneath my pants was also marred by a large crimson stain, so I knew the blood had soaked through entirely. When I finally got down to bare skin I searched frantically for any kind of open cut of my own, not an uncommon thing on the body of any NFL player. There was nothing and I was partially relieved. I did realize though that playing the game would never be quite the same for me again.

Blood is everywhere during a football game. Gaping lacerations, raw and bleeding turf burns, torn finger-nails, and bloody noses are as common as chin straps; everyone has them. You don't see a lot of this blood from your seat in the stadium or even on TV, but it's there. Any player will tell you that it's simply part of any Sunday afternoon.

Only one transmission of the virus during an athletic contest has ever been completely substantiated. During an Italian soccer match in the late 1980s two players collided head-to-head. Both bled profusely and the commingling of their blood was reported to have trans-mitted AIDS from one player to the other. Because of the widespread attention this incident received when it appeared in the British medical journal *The Lancet,* and because of the corresponding announcement by NBA all star Magic Johnson that he was infected with the AIDS virus, the NBA adopted a policy that forces bleeding players to be removed from the court until the open wound is covered and the flow of blood stopped. The NFL passed on this sensible alternative to the sug-gestion that every player in the sports world be tested for the virus and banned from playing if they were infected.

The risks are remote, so the idea of testing everyone is too intrusive, although many players themselves don't think this is the case. Most would prefer widespread testing for the AIDS virus and banning infected players from the game. The NBA's approach seems to be a sensible middle ground. They admit that the possibility exists, and have taken a practical step to take already remote odds into the realm of the infinitesimal.

The thing that bothers NFL players the most about the league's complete disregard of the issue is how the medical staffs now treat open wounds. The trainers and doctors in the NFL have been advised by the league not to handle a player's open or bleeding wound without the protection of latex gloves. So, while the more permanent fixtures of a ball club, the doctors and trainers, are walking around with surgical gloves on the sideline of a game and using good caution when exposing themselves to blood, players themselves are allowed to happily splash about in the stuff on a Sunday afternoon like a bunch of wild kids who've sprung a fire hydrant on a hot summer day.

CREATING THE
PERFECT BEAST:
STEROIDS, AMPHETAMINES,
AND HUMAN
GROWTH HORMONES

One of the main reasons performance drugs have played such a major part in the evolution of the modern football player is because the players themselves feel like they will never die. Well, maybe that's not the entire story. Maybe as much as thinking they can never die, a lot of football players think that life without football is death anyway, so what the hell? They'll do whatever it takes to be the best they can be. A lot of people, if put into the same circumstances, would take the risk. Think about it. The difference between making it in the NFL or not is often the difference between making a million dollars a year and making twenty-five thousand.

Make no mistake about it either, steroids, amphetamines, and human growth hormones each substantially increase a football player's performance productivity. They can easily make a good player great and a great player into a superstar. Steroids not only give the player added strength and body weight, they increase speed and even quickness, all essential elements in the game of football. You also might have heard of the psychological benefits of steroids: 'roid rage. Steroids are essentially a synthetic form of testosterone, the male hormone responsible for a male's secondary sexual characteristics, one of which is aggressive behavior. Heavy doses of steroids also increase a person's aggression, another essential component to the game of football. Amphetamines allow a player to perform an entire afternoon with a wide-open throttle. This drug-induced state of intensity may be the reason some of our favorite players were so tough and relentless on the football field through the years. Numerous times in my football career I've witnessed coaches unwittingly shower praise and thereby endorse players whose performances were enhanced by amphetamines. Human growth hormone became an alternative to steroids for the guys who absolutely needed to retain their size after the league made the use of steroids so much more difficult.

In the 1970s and 1980s, before steroids were banned by the NFL, their use was rampant. Players talked openly about the cycles they were on and traded information on which drugs were the best and how to get them. Likewise, the old-timers can still tell you about the enormous candy bowls filled with uppers that graced almost every NFL locker room during the 1970s. It was not uncommon for players to take the things by the handful. Even though every NFL team now closely regulates the dispersion of any prescription drugs, the players today still can get and freely use amphetamines, although I contend their use isn't nearly as prevalent as it was twenty years ago. When the league finally banned the use of steroids and began their rigorous testing for the drugs in 1987, players using the drugs went underground. Those who used to boast about their brilliant selection of drugs suddenly got quiet. Still, most didn't lose that inflated size and strength.

In January of 1993, after the NFL had declared its war on steroid use already won, two active players, Mark Duckens from Tampa Bay and Eric Moore from the New York Giants, were indicted by the DEA for trafficking steroids. When the story first broke, agents hypothesized that the indictment of Duckens and Moore was merely the beginning. The DEA had seized enough steroids from the two players to supply two complete NFL teams for an entire football season. More indictments were predicted, but the story was strangely squelched. When I talked to a DEA agent that summer, he told me that the agency's initial assessment of the amount of drugs involved was now being revised. Duckens was absolved, and Moore received a four-week suspension from the NFL before resuming his career in Cincinnati with a multimillion-dollar deal.

You wonder what players are doing with these drugs if the NFL is testing for them? To this day there are players who have found ways to beat the NFL's testing procedure. Each player is tested for steroids in an overall drug screening that is done during training camp. Then, every week thereafter, players are randomly selected for additional steroid testing. In the early days of testing, players would simply keep a plastic bottle of clean urine in their shorts, walk into the bathroom stall, and squirt the clean urine into the specimen container. The NFL got wise fast and soon began to require that lab technicians watch the players urinate in the open. Finally, the policy required the technicians to observe the player urinating from a full frontal vantage point with the player's pants pulled down to his knees, an embarrassing situation for both player and technician, but a wise move by a league determined to level the playing field.

Now, only Houdini could fake what is known as

"the piss test." However, when millions of dollars are in the balance, the human spirit knows no bounds to creativity. In 1990, a group of Philadelphia Eagles admitted to bringing a doctor in from out of town on the night before the league's annual piss test in training camp. The next morning, immediately before the test, these players, all steroid users, had the doctor catheterize clean urine into their bladders, which they in turn voided in front of the lab technicians. They all passed the test with flying colors. Many other people contend that there are masking agents available on the open market that can also prevent the detection of steroid use. This certainly seems likely. As far as the random tests go, it is not uncommon for a player randomly selected to dodge the NFL "Piss Man" until the next day, thus giving that player an opportunity to make the necessary chemical or biological alterations to pass the test. So, you see, there really is no way to completely regulate steroid use.

That said, I do believe the NFL has made a noble effort at eliminating the problem. They find out how they're being beaten at the test, and they come up with a new method. But even they will concede that a certain number of determined players will always slip through the cracks. There is currently no testing for amphetamine use during NFL games, nor is there a test used to detect human growth hormones.

As far as the health risks involved in performance drugs, of course Lyle Alzado comes to mind. After extensive use of each of the aforementioned drugs, and many more, Alzado was diagnosed with terminal brain cancer. He publicly swore that the use of those drugs was what brought about his demise and he struggled in his last remaining days to warn others like him, athletes at every level, about the perils of performance drug use. He told us all that it wasn't worth one bit of the fame, the money, the championships, and the good times. It wasn't worth it to die a slow, painful, and wasting death at what should only have been the mid-way point of his life.

I can tell you without hesitation that this man's tragic death had almost no impact whatsoever on professional football players. I never once heard a player say he would stop using performance drugs because of what happened to Lyle. Lyle used them all. Lyle used them too long. Lyle was just unlucky, it was a freak thing. I heard all the rationalizations you can imagine. The fact is, football players never think it can happen to them. But to survive in the NFL, you have to think this way, that it can never happen to you. Otherwise, every time you walked out onto the field you'd be too afraid of getting hurt to play the game the way it was meant to be played, with no holds barred.

I think it's important to mention that beyond the medical risks involved in using any of these performance drugs there is another reason they are wrong. Using these drugs is cheating. Getting away with using them is more of that common societal ill that says anything's okay so long as you don't get caught. These drugs aren't okay. They're dangerous and they're wrong. When a handful of guys get away with using performance drugs, it puts everyone else at an unfair disadvantage. I can't think of a single player I know who would want to play a game against an opponent who had one hand tied behind his back. It would be embarrassing. Yet, many are more than willing to gain an unfair advantage with the use of these performance drugs. More than anything, I think this problem is a symptom of a societal ill and not one exclusive by any means to the NFL. Somewhere along the line, we stopped caring about how the champion got to be the champion, and that's wrong. We should demand that our sports heroes play, fight, and win honestly and fairly. We should test them at every bend in the road until the problem is gone. If they don't like the testing, let them play arena football. If we did that, if we found the culprits out and stopped buying their brands of cereals and aftershaves, I promise you, we soon wouldn't have any perfect beasts.

PLAYING WITH PAIN

Pain and football are inseparable. It is part of the NFL's mystique. People marvel that men can continue to play the game, pounding, running, and struggling against other men while suffering from broken bones, torn ligaments, and damaged muscles. If you can't play with pain, you have to be one of the rare superstars to last more than a season in the NFL. Everyone gets hurt, even the quarterbacks, even, believe it or not, the kickers.

One thing every NFL player quickly learns is the difference between pain and discomfort. Discomfort is a constant state for an NFL player. There is always something nagging you, even if it's as simple as a finger that's been split open because it got caught in another player's face mask or a bruised toe that was crushed by someone's cleated shoe. Those things are discomforts. They bother you, but in the heat of practice or a game, you can temporarily forget about them. Most guys have to deal with several of these at the same time.

Pain is something altogether different. Pain is when the physical damage is so extreme that the jolting messages sent from the injured area to the brain are just too much to be ignored, even during a game when your entire focus is on doing your job and winning. Things like broken bones and separated joints are good candidates for pain. Once I watched a teammate play a game with a metal pin sticking out of his thumb. That was painful just to see. He'd broken the bone and the team surgeon put a pin in there during the week to hold the two pieces together. Because of the constant impact during the game, play after play, the pin worked itself out of the bone and right out through the skin. Ultimately the pin popped completely out but the player was home by then, having dinner. The bloody pin fell into his salad.

It is true that one man's discomfort is another man's pain. No one knows the physiological pain tolerance from one person to the next. We know though that people do have different tolerances. This doesn't mean some people can simply tough it out. This means that physiologically some people feel more pain for the exact same injuries. One thing for certain is that almost every guy I know in the NFL will play with pain. I know this because of the great lengths I've seen guys go to in order to stay out there on the field. There are things you can do to deal with pain, and most guys in the NFL will do what they can to be there for their teammates on Sunday.

My buddy with the pin in his thumb, for example. He was able to get several shots of Novocain put into his hand to help numb the pain. But when something is buried in your bone, they can't shut it off completely without taking out the use of your entire hand, so there you have it: playing with pain. The problem with all medical solutions to pain is pretty much the same. You can always knock pain out with shots and pills, but you can't always do it and keep the physical edge you need to compete on the field.

As I hinted before, not everyone has to play with pain. There are certain guys, superstars like Emmitt Smith, Reggie White, Steve Young, and Troy Aikman, who can afford to sit on the sideline because of pain. Most guys aren't in that situation though. Most guys spend their entire careers either trying to overtake some cagey veteran and get his job, or trying to outdistance themselves from a young rookie breathing down their necks for an opportunity to replace them. It's a vicious and never-ending cycle. New players are brought in each year from college, old ones are retired. In order to have any kind of lasting career by taking a job from one of the older guys and fending off the younger guys behind you, you have to play hurt. Except for the stars, there is always someone waiting in the wings who can and will take your job if you prove to the team that "you cannot be relied on week after week." (That's code for playing with pain.)

Ironically, the superstars I just mentioned, Smith, White, Young, and Aikman, are all guys who *have* played with pain, despite the fact that they could easily sit out with something as innocuous as a hangnail, then return to the field when they were comfortable without worrying about anyone infringing on their job. Yes, it's strange but true, and something to think about the next time the guy next door starts griping about how spoiled athletes are today. The fact is that most of the big-name guys in the NFL have endured pain just like the lowest-paid special teams players, even though everyone knows they certainly don't have to.

Why the Media and the Players Hate Each Other

Of course, like anything else, this isn't always true. Media and players don't always hate each other. There are exceptions. Some players and members of the media have become good friends. Some of the best people I know are members of the media. My wife is married to a member of the media. But I'll never be able to completely shake that intuition all football players have that the media are the bad guys. It goes the other way too. Some of my new counterparts can't help themselves from sneering privately at my old counterparts. They have their reasons for this animosity, as do the players.

The players' biggest gripe is that they have to bear being put down, insulted, and at times have their manhood questioned by writers and broadcasters. Sooner or later, even the greatest of athletes feels the sting of the pen or the microphone. Most members of the media have never played in the NFL. They don't know what it's like. So how can they presume to criticize? Players see the media as a lower form of life. Somewhere between the slug and the toad, nothing as erect as a man that has battled on the grassy turf of a real football game.

I confess that a very satisfying moment for me as a player was watching two of my Falcon teammates turn a writer upside down and dump him head first into a smelly trash can. He wrote some bad things about them and they ambushed him the next day in the locker room. It wasn't done good-naturedly. They hated him and they wanted to dump him into that bin of fetid, used ankle tape and oozing gobs of human expectorant. It seemed appropriate after the words the writer had spit out at them. For the first time I'd ever seen, a writer was taken to task for the things he'd written. Most times writers will verbally lambaste a player and then appear the very next day strolling through the locker room, the domain of the players, with the diplomatic immunity of a statesman from some despicable terrorist country.

Of course, the writer who got trashed was correct in his assessment of the two players who got him. Essentially he wrote that they were boobs, and he was right. They proved it further by dumping him in the trash. He was a pretty decent guy too, and I'm kind of ashamed that I enjoyed it. But it was just the notion of one of "them" getting a little medicine to go along with the stuff they are constantly dishing out that made me forget myself.

It's like a dog seeing the cat he coexisted with for years suddenly flattened under the screeching tires of a van. The dog just can't help himself from a little grin. It's in his nature. That's what it comes down to, the essential elements of nature. Players play the games. They sweat, bleed, and suffer. The media either criticizes or lauds them. If their words are laudatory, players feel they deserved it. If they are critical, players wonder how some pencil-neck could dare to even comment on something so obviously beyond his scope of experience or understanding. The problem as I see it with players is that they can't buy the hype and knock the snipe. You either have to say the media knows everything, or nothing, but you can't have it both ways, saying they're smart when they kiss you and stupid when they slap you.

For their part, the media has to endure all sorts of insults. I've seen players pointedly ignore a group of grown men while they casually stuff their privates into their underwear and dress themselves slower than any time since they were four years old, then dramatically douse themselves with sprays and colognes making the air unbearable to breathe before finally condescending to speak in sullen monotones to the cameras and microphones. Players get paid millions to do something most writers would give up a Pulitzer Prize for. They sometimes rebuff kids begging for autographs, a scenario members of the media can only dream of. They drive expensive cars, adorn themselves with flashy jewelry and women, and live in the best sections of town.

In short, to the media, the players have it made. They are given everything like spoiled children, but then ultimately most of them will squander it all and shuffle through life after their spectacular careers as nothing more than the decrepit shells of the legends they have become. Writers, on the other hand, are enduring, as is their work. They are like hardy beetles, slogging along, year after year, watching with contempt as the brilliant and enviable butterflies come and go, falling uselessly to the ground after only a brief foray into the heavens. Because of some players' bad behavior, the media despises them. Because of the players' wealth and fame, the media takes no pity.

I understand both sides and there is no right answer. As a player, I remember talking one time with a reporter about crossing the picket line during the 1987 players' strike. I talked for a half hour and espoused my reasons for what I'd done. That writer listened to me, but he didn't hear. He didn't want to. I could tell by the biting story he wrote the next day that he had no intention of using anything I said to him in defense of my actions. He called simply to be able to say that he'd spoken with me. The piece, I realized, had already been written. I was incensed and I was powerless. I wished then more than ever that I could dump someone in a trash can of my own, or better yet, that I could get that pencil-neck out on the field for just ten minutes in an Oklahoma drill where I could mash him into the dirt just to let him in on what it's really like. Instead, I swallowed hard and went on. But I never forgot what the sting of that one-sided criticism felt like. I knew then why dogs innately hate cats.

On the other side, as a current member of the media, I know the humiliation of trying to get an audience with a player whose self-importance has swollen beyond the proportions of decency. When they know me, and know that I played, players treat me differently. They will address their answers to me in a knowing way with the wink and the nod of a secret society. "You know what I mean," they'll say. I nod back because I do. If they don't recognize me, which is easy in the mob of reporters after a game, then I sometimes get the same brush-off that most of the media have felt. They don't have time to talk. Get out of their way. Strangely, the embarrassment of being the recipient of that rude behavior isn't unlike the sting of being burned by the media. So, now I know why the cats hate the dogs as well.

EATING CROW

So now, after reading the last chapter, you know how the media and the players feel about each other, and hopefully you know why. With that in mind, and with the fact that I have been in both camps, I want to tell you a story about how I've applied what I have learned.

I was broadcasting a game for FOX between the New Orleans Saints and the New York Giants with my partner, Joe Buck. All week I prepared for the game by memorizing the rosters of both teams so I would know the players by their numbers. I also read recent newspaper articles so I would know what was going on within the rank and file of each club. Part of this ingestion of information takes me right up to minutes before kickoff. I like to read the morning paper just in case I missed something during my week of research and the day I spent with the teams, Saturday, talking with the coaches and players. Usually I don't learn anything I don't already know, but it would be inept to do a game without knowing some important news item regarding either team that had emerged overnight and not be prepared to talk about it during the broadcast.

Among the articles I had read during the week, there were several that pondered the effectiveness and courage of Jim Everett, the Saints quarterback who had come from the Los Angeles Rams. In Los Angeles, Everett had acquired the reputation of having "happy feet." A quarterback is said to have happy feet if when he gets any kind of pressure in the pocket from the defensive pass rushers his feet start to skitter and jump like he's about to run away. Happy feet is more than just jumpy feet, it includes the ducking and dodging of defenders, or even the shadows of defenders, when they get anywhere close to the quarterback. A quarterback with happy feet can rarely concentrate on his receivers downfield because he is so worried about the linemen and linebackers coming after him.

Jim also acquired the reputation that because of his happy feet, he could be rendered ineffectual by blitzing him play after play. The theory was that he could be so shaken that he'd never get a good pass off. The Rams and their fans, however, forgot that it was this same quarterback that had led them to the playoffs and earned a trip to the Pro Bowl only a few years earlier. The problems in L.A. went far beyond Jim Everett, and he and his feet became the scapegoat for a struggling program. Head coach Chuck Knox did nothing to defuse this unjust portrayal of Everett either. Then, mercifully, Jim was able to get away from L.A. and land with New Orleans, a team he had decimated through the years with his passing ability, a team renowned for its bloodthirsty defenses that had enjoyed no success whatsoever in making Everett jumpy with the blitz. The short story was that the Saints players and staff swore that Everett was being unjustly miscast.

After reading about this controversy all week, I was

reminded of it once more the morning of the game. There was an extensive article recounting Jim Everett's appearance on a talk show with Jim Rome, a member of the media. Rome proceeded throughout the interview to refer to Jim Everett as "Chris" or "Chrissy" Everett, making a play on the name of the female tennis player and Jim's reputation for being less than courageous in L.A. Jim asked him to stop, then told him to stop, and finally, when Rome stubbornly continued with his insults, Everett body-slammed the TV talk host right there on the set and began pummeling him. The notion of Jim Everett, no small man and no wimp by any standard, giving this sharp-tongued reporter some medicine of his own stuck in my mind. Unfortunately, that wasn't the only thing that stuck.

The game began. Joe Buck and I talked fluidly throughout as the Giants and the Saints battled back and forth in a close contest. The Giants, who must have been reading the same papers as I, did try to send the pass rush heat after Jim Everett. Everett responded as the Saints promised he would. He stepped up, showed no fear, and picked the Giants apart with his passing skills. At one time during the excitement, when Giants tackle Mike Fox was smashing into Everett on a replay, I declared, "Watch Fox put the heat on Chris Everett—I mean Jim Everett . . ."

Of course, football writers aren't the only ones waiting to pounce. A TV sportswriter in New York picked up on my glitch and printed it in the next morning's paper. I had no opportunity to retract what I'd said or offer any kind of public apology. What was perceived as another insult hurled at Jim Everett was nothing more than a dumb mistake. I couldn't take it back, but I could say I was sorry. I called the Saints' public relations office and asked Rusty Kasmiersky, the PR director, for Jim's home phone number. I explained what had happened and told him why I was calling. He was shocked.

"You mean, you want to apologize to him?" Rusty said.

"Yes," I told him. "I think I should say it to him personally."

Rusty explained that nothing like that had ever happened.

"Usually, guys make mistakes or say something bad about guys and they just go on," he told me.

I got ahold of Jim and told him what happened.

"I'm sorry," I said. "I made a mistake. I don't have an excuse. It was a stupid thing to do and very unprofessional. I just wanted you to know."

Jim displayed the same disbelief that Rusty had.

I'm not saying that I'm better or worse than any other member of the media. All I'm saying is that players make mistakes, the media makes mistakes. We're all in the business of football together. We all love the game and we love our jobs. They're good jobs that a lot of other people wish they had. The players and the media all need to realize that they're in it together. If the players didn't put on a good show, the NFL wouldn't be the great entertaining sport that it is. If the media didn't do a good job covering it to keep people watching and caring, the NFL would lose its luster and its mystique. It's a simple rule that we all learned in kindergarten. The NFL players and media need to remember it. If you're wrong, just say you're sorry.

The Ultimate Traitor: Life in the Broadcast Booth

I remember playing linebacker against the Rams one game and having coverage in the flat. It was a pass play and I rolled out to the edge of the field about five yards deep from the line of scrimmage. There was no one in my zone and I noticed a receiver out of the corner of my eye streaking up the field. I glanced over my shoulder and saw that the cornerback had been sucked inside by another receiver and abandoned his deep zone. I turned and ran. Fortunately for our team, Jim Everett didn't put enough juice on the pass and the receiver had to come back to the ball. This enabled me to catch up to him and tackle him for a thirty-yard gain that could have been a touchdown. When I got home, my wife's face was glum. She felt bad about my being burned in pass coverage on TV. I told her not only had I not blown my coverage, but that I'd saved a touchdown. We were both incensed at the error the announcer had made in criticizing me.

Of course now, many years later, I forgive him. I have made the same kinds of mistakes myself. If I realize it, and I'm still on the air, I admit it and go on. If I don't realize it until later, there's nothing I can really do, and, unless it's a matter of personal insult as discussed in the previous chapter, I don't lose any sleep over it. You have to remember. I'm a turncoat anyway, and I know it. I've joined the other team and I'm one of the bad guys. That's okay. It has to be. It's how I make my living.

Every player who's been around for any length of time has had it happen to him. Some stiff up in the broadcast booth cuts him down. Of course when you're playing the game, you never know when it happens. But without a doubt, every player ever criticized by a broadcaster eventually hears about it. If the girlfriend or the wife or the parent or some friend wasn't watching the game on TV, then a player can always depend on some loyal fan to accost him at the grocery store or in a restaurant during the week to ask him how he feels about being called a bust or a wimp or a loser by some guy in a jacket and tie watching the game from the safety of the broadcast booth.

There are some broadcasters, John Madden for example, who believe it is inappropriate for the media to challenge the manhood of an NFL football player. I remember John during a FOX Sports production meeting distinctly saying, "I don't think it's right for anyone to say any of these guys aren't tough. We're talking about NFL football players here. You don't get to the NFL without being a tough guy and a great athlete."

John Madden is exactly right. Still, there is a pressure from people within the sports media to be critical of athletes. Strangely enough, broadcasters have critics of their own. You may not be aware of this. As a player, I never was. But broadcasters are subject to the scrutiny of television critics who write columns in almost every major newspaper across the country. Like the sports media, some are smart and fair, others are mean-spirited and less than brilliant. Both have the power to enhance or impair their subject's careers. Sports television critics demand that broadcasters tread on eggshells, with steel-toed boots. And, whether they like it or not, everyone inside the broadcasting industry is affected by what the critics write.

It is a rookie analyst's greatest fear to be perceived as unable or unwilling to criticize his former counterparts down on the field. Because of this, those players who do become members of the television media quickly lose the ability to mingle among a group of football players and be considered just one of the guys. A broadcaster is not one of the guys. He is the enemy. It is either that, or he doesn't last long as a broadcaster.

The hardest thing for me to do in my first season as a nonplayer was to talk badly about one of my best friends in the league, Hugh Millen. Hugh was backing up John Elway in Denver. Elway was down with an injury. The game was Christmas Eve day. Hugh threw a weak pass that got picked off and hurt Denver's chances for a come-from-behind victory. I gritted my teeth and said it was a poorly thrown ball. Merry Christmas. I explained that to throw that type of pass a quarterback must get the ball to the receiver's outside shoulder, away from the defender. Hugh had thrown it inside and it was a wobbling duck to boot. It hurt me to say it. When I spoke to Hugh later and apologized for doing what I felt I had to do, he told me it was all right. "Besides," he said to me, "you were right. It was a bad pass." Still, it didn't make me feel much better. My buddy was down, and I had stepped on his face.

Whether the broadcaster is right or wrong in his criticism, no player appreciates having his mistakes or shortcomings pointed out during a network telecast.

This type of finger-pointing, however, is one of the essential elements of being a broadcaster. Pointing out the errors as well as the great plays is a must for every color analyst. A broadcaster has to subordinate his concern for the ego of the players to providing an accurate description of what happened and why.

An active NFL player can never understand this. To a player, anyone who criticizes them is a fool who never played the game. What right do they have to be critical? A former player who criticizes them is a traitor. How could he talk like that when he knows what we go through? How indeed?

It's really not that hard. When you finally face the facts as an ex-football player that it's either their feelings or your job, you choose to preserve your job. I simply use the same mentality that enabled me to play in the NFL for eight years. It is an "us or them" perspective that enables you as a player to go out and try to knock opposing players off their feet, beat them into the dirt, and send them packing with their heads hung low. It is the same mentality that you have to have to keep the young rookie from taking away your job.

Same thing in broadcasting. The job puts food on the table. You do the best you can. I try to look at the positive instead of the negative. For every missed tackle, there is a good feint by the runner. For every interception thrown by the quarterback, there is a heads-up play by a defender. For every burned defensive back, there is a touchdown. Still, even the most optimistic announcer has to call a blunder a blunder and a fool a fool. Worse yet, broadcast mistakes are inevitable. No announcer can know every player's responsibility on every play.

Life goes on regardless. Players, although offended, certainly don't lose their jobs because of some mistake a broadcaster might make. If the broadcaster simply points out the obvious, and the infraction is great, it doesn't matter what is said by whom, the player will lose his job, if at all, on the merits of his mistake alone. Meanwhile, in the booth, you can either brazenly stomp on feelings, or pack your bags. I prefer the former. Just call me Benedict Green.

"DR. MEAN"

It would be hypocrisy for me to denounce the San Francisco 49ers' offensive line coach, Bob McKitrick. On the other hand, I would be remiss for not letting you in on what every defensive lineman in the NFL for the past fifteen years has known. In my opinion he is the NFL's meanest coach. I can see his smile as I write. He doesn't care what people call him, me or anyone else for that matter. He doesn't care that Howie Long has denounced him publicly. He doesn't care if you don't send him a Christmas card or smile cheerfully when he walks through the door. He is the quintessential football coach, the kind of man nightmares and championships are made of. If Vince Lombardi was alive, I promise you, he would have wanted Bob McKitrick as his offensive line coach.

So, how can I admire a man I reviled as a player, a man I call "Dr. Mean"? It's easy. I don't have to face his questionable tactics anymore, and I can admit that if I were a 49er fan, quarterback, running back, offensive lineman, owner, or coach, I would love this man for what he's done for the team.

The 49er offensive line is relentless in their blocking. By that I mean that beyond the conventional methods of smashing into you to knock you out of the way, they will hook you, grab you, pull you, punch you, kick you, leg-whip you, or dive at the back of your knees in their effort to keep you out of a play. The biggest complaints that opposing players have is the consistent use of leg whips and roll-up blocks. A leg whip is when the offensive lineman dives forward, past his defensive adversary, and whips his leg backward at the defensive player's shin or knee, heel first. The result can be crippling, as was the case with Denver Broncos middle linebacker Karl Mecklenberg, or at least painful, as is the case almost every time the 49ers take the field. A roll-up block takes place when the defensive lineman has somehow gotten past the blocker and is on his way to the ball carrier. The offensive lineman then dives at the back of the defender's knees and rolls sideways as he makes contact. The effect is like a steamroller crawling up the back of a signpost. The post always bends. It always goes down. Sometimes it breaks.

There has been some back-and-forth speculation as to why some of the 49er linemen are reputed to throw these two kinds of blocks on a consistent basis. Some people say they are coached that way. Some people deny that.

How bad are these techniques? It depends on who you are. If you're used to the Ivy Leagues and suddenly people are flying at your knees while you're trying to play a game of football, they're pretty bad. If you're used to the brutal style of football that can erupt between bitter rivals of inner-city high school teams or mutually hateful college programs, then this kind of stuff only makes you curse and tighten up your chin strap. No one has ever officially chastised the 49ers for this behavior even though everyone with their head above the sand knows it's going on. The 49er offensive line doesn't draw more penalties than any other offensive line. Some would contend that means there's no problem. I contend that means they're simply getting away with it.

That's something to think about. When Jerry Glanville was the coach of the Falcons he used to say, "If you ain't cheatin', you ain't tryin'." That happens almost every play during a game. Offensive players will hold defensive ones. Defensive players will use illegal head slaps and grab face masks. Coaches will try to steal signals from their opponents and intercept plays going into the huddle. Players covertly replace rubber cleats with metal baseball spikes for better footing. Linemen and runners sometimes spray their jerseys with silicone so opponents slip off like a well-done egg on a Teflon griddle. Basically, all's fair in love and war and you're not doing anything wrong unless you get caught.

It's not that bad, really. Even if there are a few teeth marks and punches and leg whips, no one has ever used any kind of weapon on a football field. It's still a primitive battle of bone and flesh with a little plastic for padding. And, when you look back at it, despite all the curses you devoted to "Dr. Mean" while you were playing, you realize that he is nothing more to the NFL than a corporate raider is to Wall Street. He's ruthless. Sometimes people get hurt. On the other hand, he's successful, and not doing anything that appears to be illegal. Otherwise he'd be in jail, right? Besides, this isn't life or death. No one is getting killed.

Strangely, in the end, we admire Bob McKitrick for the very same reasons opposing linemen hate him. He appears to be just like everyone else. He's quite pleasant actually. Yet in a sport where coldhearted violence is a good thing, even the bad guys are scared of him. He's like Clint Eastwood in an old Western, and we like that. He stands apart, and he's not afraid. He lives by his own rules. This is all great, and fun to watch, just so long as we're in the stands or at the movie theater, and not out on the field being ground up by his minions or in the Old West, being gunned down in the streets of Largo.

KICKERS AND CLUB MED

I cannot remember the exact game, or even the name of the kicker when we lost a close game one fall day in college. But I do remember the words of my defensive line coach, George O'Leary.

"Damn kickers," he said with his distinct Long Island sneer that players routinely tried to mimic after a few Saturday night beers, "all they gotta do is go out there and swing their damn leg.

"They got one job to do," he continued, "and half the time they miss and lose the damn game for you."

This was not the first time I had heard my coach rebuke kickers as a race. (Of course, if Coach O'Leary didn't admonish you, then you never felt like you were really part of the team anyway.) But my sagacious old coach is not alone in his particular distaste for kickers. The fact is that most football players and coaches consider the kicker to be nothing more than a soccer player in a football helmet.

That is, of course, until the game is on the line and the kicker blasts a fifty-plus-yard field goal in the last seconds to win the game. Then, magically, as if the kicker suddenly materialized from nowhere, he is the hero that everyone wants to clap on the back and congratulate. It must be hard to be so unappreciated. Hard, not only because it is a rare occasion when a kicker gets the opportunity to be the hero, but because every opportunity to be the hero is also an opportunity to be the ultimate goat. If the kicker misses that last-second kick, despite its distance, everyone forgets about their own fumbles and interceptions and missed tackles and blocks throughout the game. Instead, everyone heads to the locker room thinking that all the kicker had to do was make the kick and the game was won.

But it's easy for us to punish the kicker so. The fact is that he takes so little punishment when the rest of us are suffering through the trials that are part of the game that we feel not only justified, but moral in our disdain. In the NFL, the kickers' day is called Club Med. They arrive at practice later than anyone else and are the first to leave. While the rest of us are propping our eyes open in two-hour film sessions and cramming blackboards full of game plans into our heads, the kickers are taking a nice long Jacuzzi while leisurely reading *USA Today*. During training camp, while the rest of us stagger about under the painful aches in our muscles and joints and meet until all hours of the night, the kickers are bopping down to the mall to catch a movie or fritter away their time on video games.

So it's easy to see why kickers are outcasts. In the NFL, the kicker and the punter are a team unto themselves. They have no position coach and no players who also do what they do. They room together on the road, eat together, and as far as I know they open Christmas presents together too. By the time kickers reach the NFL though, they are comfortable with these facts. They do their own thing and disregard the rest.

What made me nervous at times was that I always seemed to get along with the kickers so well. In the NFL, I found myself having more in common with them than with many of my other teammates. (If someone else said that to me it would be an insult, but I can say it about myself.)

The truth is though that there are kickers who are just tough, mean football players. They simply got stuck in a body that was too slow or too short or too light, but they just refused to leave the football field. These are the guys that everyone loves, guys like Kevin Butler from the Bears. One year, I saw him body-slam our toughest special teams player during a kickoff. The guy's name was Brick if that's any indication. Brick went after Butler licking his chops, thinking he was just another kicker. At the last second, Butler turned, smashed Brick in the mouth with a forearm, and tossed him to his back. I think if you'd ask Kevin Butler, he'd say he was meant to play on the line. He's just a street fighter who happens to be able to kick the football.

So you can't give a qualified no if someone asks you are kickers really football players. Some of them have hearts as big as the meanest of linebackers. But let's not get carried away . . . when football is at its worst, when the sweat is stinging your eyes, when the fatigue is making you nauseous, when blood is running down your smashed and sticky fingers, a football player can always look up and see the kicker, off by himself, on some nearby patch of cool grass, and of course, he is simply standing there, swinging his damn leg.

THOSE BORING MEETINGS

You have to understand that despite all the glorious excitement of playing in the NFL, much of the way a player spends his time is painfully boring. The workday during the season is typically nine to five, and although the team gets let out for practice (a school recess of sorts), the majority of the day is spent in meetings. They are boring beyond description. Granted, there is much to learn about the upcoming opponents and their tendencies and the plays you will use against them. Timing on the football field is critical and everyone has to be at the right place at the right time in order to be victorious. But the fact remains that even the most intricate strategies are not as difficult as, say, learning integral calculus, and most of the calculations regarding the behavior of the other team are typically thrown out after the first few plays of the game. Teams tend to change what they do from week to week.

I was of the sentiment that football in the NFL could be much simpler than it was made out to be. Ultimately, the game comes down to the basics of blocking, tackling, running, catching, and throwing. These are things that can only be learned or improved on during recess, or practice. Unfortunately, because of the nature of the sport, day-long practices are not productive. People get hurt. People get fatigued. And since everyone's job security is determined by what happens on Sunday, no one is keen on the idea of using up too much energy or luck during the week of practice. What I'm saying is that you can only practice so long, and most teams make up the difference in the day by poring over computer readouts on tendencies of the opposition, and watching the same reels of film over and over again, specifically, film of the opponents in their last three or four contests.

Meetings begin at the outset of the day, then continue until a short lunch. After lunch, it's more meetings until practice. Then when practice is over, there are usually more meetings before players are free to go home. Every meeting is presided over by at least a position coach, if not a coordinator or the head coach himself. Missing a meeting results in a thousand-dollar fine. Being late will typically cost you two hundred. There are no excuses either. A broken-down car, auto accident, traffic jam, or even sickness won't get you out from under a fine for being late or missing a meeting.

The idea behind all these film meetings is that players will know the way the opponents think better than the opponents themselves, and that the players will somehow anticipate what is going to happen and thereby be at the right place at the right time quicker than if they hadn't watched game film all week. The reality is that a lot of guys daydream or sleep during these meetings. Some players make no bones about the fact that as soon as the lights go off they are going to slumber. They make themselves comfortable, stretch their legs, lean their heads against the wall, and even pull their caps down before the lights are even off. If the player is good enough, and his job is completely se-cure, the only time his sleep will be interrupted by a coach is if his snoring becomes too loud.

For some reason I could never allow myself to sleep during a meeting. Even during the years of my career when my job was relatively safe, even when my eyes were sagging and my head was drooping from having stayed out too late the night before, I just could never bring myself to allow sleep to take over. There were times I would have liked to sleep and times I was envi-ous of those who could. I guess it was my upbringing that would never allow me to be comfortable with sim-ply falling asleep when my immediate boss was right there.

I wasn't, however, what you'd call a model student during those boring meetings. Although I remained awake, there were times my mind was crawling with desperation for something to do. I couldn't shake the notion that I was wasting so many valuable hours of the day, just sitting there after already having absorbed the lessons for the week. To keep myself sane, I did two things. I began by reading. When I got caught, I started writing. I fashioned a small penlight with an aluminum foil screen over the end so that I could sit in the back of a large meeting room and direct a small beam of light on a few sentences at a time. Reading was something I would only do when the film being watched or the strategy being explained had nothing to do with me. This would happen all the time in special teams meet-ings.

Practically the entire team would be in these meet-ings because almost everyone had at least a minor role in the special teams. It was often the case that the film and the discussion was about something that had noth-ing to do with me, like the kickoff return, a team I wasn't on. Other guys would grow restless as well. Doughnuts

and spitballs flying through the gloom weren't an uncommon sight. During these times, I would pull out my
light and whatever book I happened to be reading, and
have at it.

One day Foge Fazio, the former head coach at Pitt
and then Falcons special teams coach, pulled me aside
after a meeting. He'd caught me. Foge was always a
great guy and he didn't make a big deal about it. I was
embarrassed anyway (not as much as if I'd been sleeping), and I promised to retire my light.

After battling boredom for several weeks during
these long interludes of darkness, I conceived an idea
that would enable me to occupy my mind and be free
from reproach. I began writing, not with a computer,
but by thinking about the material I would put down
that night when I was back at home. I would jot notes
in the margins of my game plan and on the backs of
pages in my playbook, tearing off corners or even entire pages where I had scribbled ideas and scenarios in
the weak light of the film projector. My desk at home
was constantly piled with scraps of paper that I would
consult late into the night while composing newspaper
articles, radio commentaries for NPR, or pages and
scenes of whatever was my current novel.

Because there were times when I would drift off into
my own literary world during these film sessions, my
defensive line coach, Bill Kolar, thought I was a veritable idiot. He would ask me questions from time to time
when my mind was miles away. Oftentimes I wouldn't
even hear his questions. He would chortle at these un-
responsive moments and declare that certainly there
was no correlation between having done well as a student, and the everyday common sense it took to func-
tion in life. "You're so smart with books, you're
stupid," he would tell me. I would dutifully absorb his
technical football point with a smile so as not to make

a mistake during Sunday's game, then drift pleasantly back into my own world of words.

I know football coaches everywhere will sneer at this revelation, but it's the truth. Players just can't sit all day in a dark room and maintain complete fascination with tiny figures pushing, pulling, and darting at one another on a screen. In my own defense, although my mind may not have always been on the meeting at hand, at least my eyes were open.

What Is the Salary Cap, and Why Do Most Players Hate It?

The salary cap is the limit on how much each NFL team can spend on its players' salaries each season. The first year it was imposed, 1994, the limit was $34.6 million. In 1995, the limit was $37.1 million. The amount is equal to 63 percent of what the league calls its DGR, or designated gross revenue. This is money received from television, radio, and gate receipts. The players share in this revenue, but not in other revenue sources like luxury boxes, parking, concessions, club seats, and the enormous cash cow: licensing. There is also a minimum amount that teams must spend on players' salaries, 50 percent of a team's DGR, to ensure that the historically cheaper teams like Cincinnati and Pittsburgh still dish out a substantial part of their revenue to players.

In exchange for getting free agency from the owners, the players' severance package was cut by more than half, and their meaningless pension plan remained that way. Owners, meanwhile, couldn't be happier. They now have a fixed cost on players' salaries, so fans can't complain that they are cheap, and they still bring in a tremendous amount of revenue from things like licensing that they don't have to share with the players at all.

The new free agency system in the NFL allows players to go to any team, i.e., the highest bidder, after the first four years of their contract with the team that drafted them out of college. The reason there is a cap, or limit on the amount teams can spend on salaries, is so that big-money-making teams like Dallas and the New York Giants can't outbid the other teams by having $50 million payrolls and attracting all the best players. Free agency was something that most players wanted, until they realized what it would effectively do: create a system where the top 20 percent of the guys got paid the vast majority of the money. Most players in the NFL now make less than ever while the few at the top make more than ever.

The Dallas Cowboys' 1995 team is a good example. The top eleven players in Dallas used up $25 million of the cap. That left $12 million for the other forty-two men on the roster. That's an average salary of $2.3 million for the "haves," and $280,000 for the "have-nots." Granted, it's still a lot of money, but the discrepancy is huge and it makes the majority of the players quite bitter. It is not uncommon for one of the big-money players to get hurt and have a minimum-salaried guy fill in and do the same job for one tenth of the money.

Under the old system, players who were consistently productive over their careers could look forward to a gradually increasing salary where they made the bulk of their money in later years. Now, these older veterans, many of whom have provided an example of hard work and dedication for young guys, played with injuries, and devoted their free time to community service, are finding themselves either cut, or asked to play for the minimum salary so that the few marquee name players can get their big paychecks and the payroll can still fit under the cap. It only takes some simple math to understand why the substantial majority of NFL players are extremely disgruntled with the salary cap.

The days of the middle class in the NFL are all but gone. Teams' rosters are now out of necessity loaded with minimum-salary players, young and old. It's why you saw former stars who grew old, guys like Phil Simms, retiring after being offered a job for only a couple hundred thousand dollars a year. It's why in 1993, anticipating the need for a pool of low-paid players, only *eleven* rookies who were drafted that year did not make an NFL roster. That was the first time in the history of the NFL that so many young players were held on to. Young low-round draft choices are the cheapest players around, and teams are keeping them more than ever to fill in the gaps after paying off the marquee players. Creating a free agency system while simultaneously imposing a salary cap was like bringing a tray of ten cupcakes to a class of thirty kids. Ten kids are gobbling down cakes and licking their fingers with delight, while the other twenty look on, licking their chops and scrambling for the crumbs.

READING BOOKS IN THE NFL

I have spent years explaining to people on both sides of the intellectual fence that books and football have more in common than most people initially would think. Writing books and playing football both require discipline and perseverance. Both require the passionate expression of deep-seated emotions. For those who enjoy watching football and reading books, both are wonderful forms of entertainment and adventurous escape from a world that is often complex and disturbing.

Still, people immersed in the world of books, and people from the world of football look at each other with wary distrust. Someone who crosses this boundary on a daily basis is a strange bird indeed.

That's how I felt when I first got to the NFL, like a strange bird. Gone were the classes and academic requirements of college that made it understandable to football players why one of their own would constantly have his nose in a book. There is no required reading in the NFL. Still, I don't think there was a day in my career when there wasn't a book in my locker

113

that I was actively reading. During lunch breaks, or the small moments between meetings, or in the time between getting dressed and practice, on the training table while my ankles were being taped, I would read. Why not? It wasn't that I wouldn't talk with my teammates, I would. If someone wanted to talk, I would always put down my book and often this was the case. But instead of staring into space, sitting there at my locker, waiting for the horn to sound marking the time to go out on the field for practice, I would read. On the team bus, on the plane, in the hotel room, I would read.

I saw nothing wrong with this, but some people did. My books would draw looks of disgust and suspicion from some coaches and players. In the moments before a game, when anxiety is boiling up like an unwatched pot, I would retreat to the sanctity of some literary tale. This was a habit I acquired as a high school wrestler. I was the type of athlete who would be physically ill from the anxiety of the upcoming contest. My adrenaline would run high hours before the match, and exhaust my supply of this natural amphetamine long before I needed it to compete. To combat this, I would read, transporting myself into another place and time. It became almost a form of meditation, and the calm, I liked to think, before the storm. When I got out onto the mat or the football field, the emotions of the contest would come rushing out in a surge of incendiary enthusiasm. It's just the way I was. Some guys would listen to hard rock. Some guys would bang their heads against their lockers. I would read Charles Dickens.

I never thought of myself as better or worse than anyone else because of my method of preparing for a game, just different. I knew, however, in fact I was told, that reading a book in the locker room, dressed in my full NFL uniform, only minutes before kickoff on a

Sunday afternoon, was unacceptable. So, on game day, I went into hiding. I'd tape up, pull on all my gear, then disappear into the back room where the equipment manager kept the extra socks, jocks, and jerseys. Clumsily I would open my book with thick leather-gloved hands. My fingers, fraught with nervous energy, would tremble as I turned the thin sheets of paper, adorned with words. After a few minutes my mind would be free from the turmoil of the imminent contest, submerged in the story as if it were an opiate.

When Jerry Glanville came to Atlanta to coach the Falcons five years into my career, I thought my books would be burned. Glanville had a reputation for bounty hunting players whose behavior off the field had earned them criminal records instead of college degrees. I remember telling my wife there was no way I would fit in with the new regime. To my surprise, Glanville, a man who swears to this day that he won't read anything that doesn't come with a set of crayons, loved the idea that one of his players was odd enough to read books moments before a game. So, out came my books. It seemed to be one of Jerry's most delightful moments as coach of the Falcons when he found me at my locker before a big game with the 49ers (the one year we beat them twice and went to the playoffs) reading *War and Peace*, one of the most prodigious novels in print. I never heard the end of it.

The thing that Jerry cared about was how much a player gave of himself on the field. If you gave your all, or "spilled your guts" as Jerry would say, I don't think he would have cared if you wore women's underwear underneath your uniform. It's funny how the NFL works sometimes. It took a man in a black hat and a belt buckle as big as a salad plate who drives race cars in his spare time and rides a Harley to work to tell me that it was okay to read a book.

The Mob and the NFL:
Perfect Partners

When Christmas is over for the retailers, the holiday season is just gearing up for bookies and the mob. January is when the big money really starts to drop. With the Super Bowl just weeks away, bets are being waged on who and by how much on the most heavily gambled upon sporting event in human history. Funny way to think about the game of all games isn't it? But it's true. The dichotomy between organized crime's gambling operations and NFL football is as mutually beneficial as the symbiosis between human beings and *E. coli* bacteria.

When I played in the NFL, I was naive. I thought nothing could be further from the heavy-handed guys you had to deal with to get your concrete in New York City and the pristine institution of the National Football League, home to so many childhood dreams. In fact, it was the league's own preoccupation with organized crime and their determination to keep the two distinct and separate that alerted me to the frightening juxtaposition of the two. It was in the annual league-mandated meetings that I first learned about the perils

116

of gambling and the kind of company it could attract. Every year we would sit there for an hour-long meeting in the middle of August training camp. We were tired and sore. We wanted nothing more than to be left alone and hobble back to our rooms for some sleep at the end of another miserable day. But, after eight years in Atlanta with the Falcons, and having a natural propensity to pay attention in any kind of classroom setting where something new can be learned, the message finally lodged in my brain and I still can't shake it loose. The mob is out there, watching and waiting for someone to make a mistake. The FBI said it, not me.

So, naturally, I started to wonder, what if? What if someone really did get himself into the very predicament we were being warned to stay away from? Could it happen? Sure, otherwise, why all the fuss? So, I set out to write a novel about how it would happen if in fact it really did.

The name of my book is *Titans*. It is the story of Hunter Logan. He plays quarterback for the New York Titans, an NFL team that has just won the Super Bowl. Like many professional athletes, Hunter is a gambler. The mob finds out that he has been betting on NFL games through a friend. Harmless, right? Except the mob knows, and Hunter knows from his annual meeting that if the league finds out about his indiscretions, his newly signed sixteen-million-dollar contract, his Nike endorsements, and his career will be brought to a screeching halt. Hunter Logan rationalizes the situation in the same way that almost every athlete who has been involved in a fix does: He won't lose the game, he'll just take a couple points off the score. No harm, no foul. Hunter Logan jumps out of the fire and into the pan. The stakes are raised and extortion turns to kidnapping and murder.

Fiction, absolutely, but what makes it so possible?

Just this: Big-time athletics is a spawning ground for gambling. Pete Rose, Art Schlichter, Tulane, Boston College, the Black Sox are all just tips of the iceberg. What's going on below the surface is the ceaseless rolling of dice, flipping of cards, and the challenge of who can pick the best team and by how much. I've seen players lose five thousand dollars in poker on a flight from Atlanta to San Francisco, then win back ten thousand rolling dice on the way home. I've seen a player win a thousand dollars for being the first to toss a used battery into a hole in the concrete tunnel wall at Soldier Field. Me? Well, even I have won or lost a case of beer or two betting on my alma mater, Syracuse, in a Saturday gridiron contest against the alma mater of one or another of my teammates.

The why is simple. Athletes are programmed to compete and to win. It's a buzz in the brain that can't be turned off. The better the athlete, the bigger the buzz. The gambler's mentality is not only supported, but fostered by the very nature of competitive athletics. All athletes are vulnerable, football players more than anyone. Every time a football player walks out onto the field, be it for a practice or a game, it's like rolling the bones. Each new play could be the ace that begins the hot streak that leads to the Pro Bowl, or the deuce that ends a career with a debilitating injury. There is no gamble like playing the game of football, where so many other elite athletes are coming at you from every direction and are actually intent on hurting you physically.

And the answer, of course, like so many other answers, can be found in simple education. The policelike warnings for athletes to stay away from Las Vegas and shady characters with thick Brooklyn accents is well and good. But were a *Titans* scenario to actually happen, at the heart of the problem would be the commonplace addiction of an athlete to gambling. Players don't think there is anything wrong with gambling, and maybe there isn't. It's like spice for the soup. People seem to enjoy their sporting events more when a dash of cash is in the balance. But for the athletes themselves, they need to know that gambling, like alcohol, can only be safely enjoyed by the right people, at the right place, in the right time. Players already plugged into the nerve center of the action need to be educated to the perils of gambling in any way, even on the team plane, not merely sequestered from a few hot spots like Vegas, Atlantic City, and various cruise ships.

By the way, I like the Cowboys and the Dolphins this year, Dallas by 8.

WHAT STATISTICS CAN TELL YOU ABOUT THE GAME

Statistics are supposed to be able to tell us almost anything. There are statistics on how long you will live and even how you will die. We know that the average family has 2.6 kids. Who has 2.6 kids? Nowhere are statistics more prevalent in their use and nowhere are they more revered than in sports. They're everywhere in the game of football. There are statistics on how many balls a receiver catches. That's easy. There are also statistics on how many times a defensive player "pressured" the quarterback. What exactly does that mean? No one knows.

The thing is, with all these statistics floating around out there, I ask myself, what do they all really mean? Nothing.

The fact is, a statistic never won a single ball game. Sometimes numbers you think mean something good are the direct result of a team doing bad. Take passing yardage in a game. If Neil O'Donnell throws for three hundred yards and the Jets lose, it doesn't mean Neil necessarily had a great day. If one team gets up on another by any appreciable score, they'll start playing a soft zone on defense. A soft zone allows the opponent to throw wildly around the field. The whole object is to not give up the long pass, everything else is easy pickings. For the team that's losing, the battle is against the clock as much as their oppressors. They have no choice but to start throwing the ball on every play. So a big number of yards in passing may mean nothing more than that that team played poorly enough to get way behind.

People try to use statistics to figure out how good players are too. It's ridiculous. The speed test in the world of football is the forty-yard dash. How many times do you see a football player run a forty-yard dash on a straight line during a play? And do you ever see them take off their pads to do it? Speed with your football pads on and off are two entirely different things. What about the vertical jump? The only thing you need the vertical jump for on the football field is to dunk the ball over the goal post like Alvin Harper. A better question than that is, what good is the bench press statistic? If any player is lying flat on his back in the middle of the football field in the same position as when you bench-press, how good can he be in the first place?

Sometimes players have a lot of touchdowns because they get the ball whenever their team is on the goal line. Some players make interceptions because they can leap higher than others on those meaningless Hail Mary passes. (Maybe the place for the vertical jump?) Some guys have a ton of tackles because their defense is so bad that everyone runs all over them. Some defensive linemen get lots of sacks because the secondary has left no open receivers, and some secondary players get burnt on a lot of touchdowns because there is no pass rush from the linemen. What about the defensive guy who draws a double team? He doesn't make as many

tackles or sacks. Do we give him a share of his teammates' big plays?

In Chicago two seasons ago there was a time during
the season when Erik Kramer's record as the starting
quarterback for the Bears was 1-4. When Steve Walsh
was the starter, the Bears were 4-0. What did it mean?
Nothing. Those two guys had almost the same ability.
How do I know? At the time, their statistics were the
same. Eh-hum, well, let me say this anyway. Kramer
lost a game that season on Halloween night. He was
facing a veritable hurricane and a brutally tough Green
Bay defense, quarterback hell. The next week Walsh
won the game for Chicago. He got to lead the troops
against a Tampa Bay defense that threatened to get
fined for unsportsmanlike softness. The sun was shin-
ing and it was eighty-six degrees, quarterback heaven.
So you see, even the statistic of winning and losing can
mean nothing.

I'm tired of all these statistics. Forget them and just
watch the game. You can make them say anything you
want. Did you know guys who went to school west of
the Mississippi catch 1.7 more passes per game than
guys from the east? Did you know if you eat meatloaf
on Thursday night, you're seven times more likely to
force a fumble on Sunday than if you eat chicken on
Friday? What does it all mean? Nothing.

Why Every Ex-Coach Gets Back-Stabbed

When a coach loses his job in the NFL, he becomes fair game for the players and coaches he left behind. It doesn't even matter how successful they were. Except for Jimmy Johnson, whose record was unassailable, things can always be better for a team, or so players think. Remember Denver when John Elway denounced Coach Dan Reeves? Things were going to change in Denver after they got rid of Reeves, the hard-ass. Things changed all right. Denver went into a tailspin.

It doesn't matter how beloved a coach is while he's with a team, as soon as it's evident that his career is sinking, the rats start to jump ship. It's not a bad idea to abandon ship either. Remaining loyal to a coach who's no longer with a team is tantamount to refusing to bow to a medieval usurper. A new reigning king has little tolerance for those who remain loyal to the old regime. More often than not, it's off with their heads.

For this reason, you'll almost always see players scrambling to decry the outgoing coach for every ill. Dan Reeves, for instance, was too hard. Ray Handley was too soft. Jerry Glanville was too crazy. Tom Flores was too sane. Chuck Knox didn't like quarterbacks enough. Rich Kotite liked them too much. Buddy Ryan wasn't nice enough to his players. Sam Wyche is too nice. It doesn't matter who the coach is. It doesn't matter what he was really like. The fact is, if he loses, a coach is going to be fired, and before his house is even on the market, he's guaranteed to feel a cold, long blade being plunged into the spot between his ribs and his shoulder blade.

Taking the Needle:
The NFL's Purple Heart

Taking the needle is something NFL players are proud to have done. It is a badge of honor, not unlike the military's Purple Heart. It means you were in the middle of the action and you took a hit. Taking the needle in the NFL also lets everyone know that you'd do anything to play the game. It demonstrates the complete disregard for one's well-being that is admired in the NFL between players.

There are obvious physiological reasons for pain. Pain lets us know that something is wrong. We have injured our bodies in a way that demands attention. Pain is a warning to proceed with care, that more damage is imminent if the dangerous activity is not curtailed or arrested altogether. Novocain or Xylocaine, or whatever kind of canes the doctors use to numb the human body, is a prevalent part of life in the NFL. As I said, players admire peers who take a shot of Xylocaine before a game. It is a certain sign of toughness and lets everyone know that that player can be counted on to "do whatever it takes."

I would have taken a needle. I even tried to get one

once. The time I separated my collarbone, I begged for
the needle. There were only five weeks to go in the season and I was in the last year of my first contract. Each
of the prior three years I'd spent time on injured re-
serve. I knew that it was essential for me to play despite
the separated bone if I was to avoid the permanent
stigma of being injury-prone. The pain was severe and I
was going to play no matter what. So, I reasoned, why
not take a needle and make it manageable? The team
doctors wouldn't give it to me though. They said the
area in question was too close to my heart and lungs to
risk injecting the drug.

In one way, I am ashamed to say I never took a needle. I never got to show my teammates that I would
make what is thought of as the ultimate sacrifice for
the good of the team. Now that life in the NFL is behind me I could proclaim with condescension that I
was too smart to have allowed something like that to
happen to me, that I saw the big picture and that certainly I knew playing in one game of football wasn't
worth the real risk of permanent and serious injury to
my body. But if I said that, and acted like that, I would
be lying. I wasn't that smart, even though I knew the
story of someone who took the needle and will pay for
it for the rest of his days.

The Falcons had a safety in the late 1980s whose
name was Bret Clark. Bret was an All-America from
Nebraska who had taken the route to the NFL through
the USFL, which was fairly common at that time. He
was one of the players who got more money for playing in the now defunct league than he was being offered by NFL teams. During his final NFL season Bret
injured his knee.

Now, you have to know a little bit about knee injuries before we go on. Most doctors will admit that
the real extent of a knee injury is uncertain until they

actually open you up with a knife and go inside. Even with the advent of the MRI, which is supposed to give doctors an accurate three-dimensional image of the inside of the knee, things are still quite uncertain. In the late 1980s, before MRIs were in vogue, there were three ways physicians could evaluate the damage done to an injured knee.

First, there was, and still is, the manual manipulation of the joint to test for pain and loose ligaments. I can tell you that I've seen doctors proclaim players to be perfectly fine after one of these examinations when it was ultimately discovered that the player's entire knee was destroyed. When I say destroyed, I mean "The Terrible Triad" where the anterior cruciate ligament, the medial collateral ligament, and the cartilage have all been torn. I've also seen it go the other way, where the doctor determined that the knee was ruined and subsequently found to be merely sprained or bruised. Second, there was a procedure called an arthrogram, where the knee was injected with dye and then X-rayed. To the layman, the accuracy of this procedure seemed to be dubious at best. Finally, a doctor might have chosen to do an exploration with an arthroscope, which was a surgical invasion but would give the best indication of what was really going on inside the joint.

It was by one of the aforementioned methods that it was determined Bret Clark had damaged the cartilage in his knee. It was also determined that he could continue to play despite the pain and difficulty he had in even walking on his knee. At first, Bret would try to practice, using ice and anti-inflammatories to battle the imminent swelling from putting that kind of strain on his already damaged joint. At the end of the week, on Sunday mornings, his knee would be drained.

If you have never had your knee drained, you should know that it's not as easy as turning on the tap of a keg and letting the contents spill out. When a knee fills with fluid, it looks like a puffy grapefruit. When you touch it, it squishes, not unlike a miniature waterbed. That fluid, one of the body's protections against overusing an injured joint, prevents the full range of motion, which disables the person from running or even walking without a limp. To extract this pale, clear yellow fluid, a large needle (this horse needle seems no smaller than a cocktail straw when it's going in your knee) is inserted in the side of your knee and forced deep into the joint, all the way under your kneecap. The pain is excruciating. The plunger is extracted and, like a fat plastic mosquito, the syringe slowly bubbles as it is filled with the yellow fluid, which is sometimes swirling with diluted crimson clouds of blood. Bret would have this done every Sunday. And then, immediately after the draining, smaller needles would be used to strategically inject the Xylocaine that would mercifully numb his knee.

As the weeks passed, his limp during the week became more pronounced. He would practice less and less, until finally he didn't practice at all. Bret would sit in the meetings and absorb all he could about what was going to happen. He would have to mentally run through practice reps that backup players would actually perform. He could play without practicing. He was that good. He took the needle every week. He was that tough. Everyone marveled at the pain and obvious physical damage this young man endured in the name of winning. He was a team player, an example to us all.

Then, one Sunday morning, the horse needle produced nothing more than a viscous red goop. With no fluid coming out, the swelling could no longer be controlled. Although Bret took the needle once again and tried to gimp out there with the rest of the team, it was no use. The swelling in the joint would not permit him to perform. His body had finally defeated the wiles of modern medicine.

That was the end of Bret Clark's career. He was finished with the NFL and the NFL was finished with him. They operated and tried to clean up the mess, but his knee was already ruined. The cartilage that was causing the swelling in his knee week after week was torn. Like a loose flake of metal in a gear box, the rest of the joint slowly but surely degenerated, grinding itself down into useless gears.

The last I heard of Bret was that he was living somewhere in suburbia with his wife and kids. His knee will always be a problem. The teammate who spoke to him told me that he was having trouble just playing in the front lawn with the kids. I wonder when he explains to them what happened how he will describe it. I wonder if his Purple Heart leaves him feeling proud, or despondent.

SPEEDING TICKETS AND TABLES BY THE KITCHEN: LOSING IN THE NFL

Losing in the NFL is like an infection that quickly spreads to every area of your life. When you play for a losing team, no one wants to know you. I know this feeling well. In my eight years as an NFL player, I experienced only one season where we were winners. I remember one time, after yet another Falcon loss, going with my wife to the drive-thru window of the bank.

"They know me here," she said, "and they know who you are."

I slouched down in the seat so they might not see me, fearful of evoking pity or disdain, the two standard reactions people have to a loser. I preferred anonymity. The same thing went for dinner reservations. I would put them under my wife's maiden name. The one year we had a good season and went to the playoffs, my name was good for the best table in the house, along with a complimentary bottle of wine. During the down years, if they knew I was a player, they'd make me wait for an hour, then seat us next to the kitchen. The lowest point of my career was when our team started the season out 0-5. It was miserable. Things were so bad they even affected the way I drove my car. I had to be more careful than normal. If your team is a winner, and you get stopped for speeding, odds are the cop will ask for your autograph, and happily tell you to have a nice day. But if you get pulled over at 0-5, not only will you get hit for speeding, you're apt to get another ticket for a bad muffler or something.

Even our kids were affected by the poor record our team put forth every year. Leftover Falcon T-shirts and jerseys, displayed proudly during the one year we did win, had to be discarded, or hidden until better times. One teammate of mine wouldn't let his kids wear their Falcon clothes to the mall.

"The only way any kid would wear Falcon stuff in Atlanta," he explained to me, "is if their daddy is a player. I don't want people to see my kids and recognize who I am."

Other teammates would cringe if their kids were wearing team colors at the breakfast table. They'd implore their wives not to let the young ones go to school with anything bearing the Falcon emblem. They didn't want the kids to draw attention to the fact that their dads played for the losing team.

"Kids can be cruel," one guy told me. "I don't want my son getting picked on, or getting into fights."

If it sounds like we had a complex, it's because we had a complex. You see, losing makes you paranoid. Our society doesn't accept losing. And when it happens, everyone knows that heads will roll. At every level we discount our losing athletes. From high school to the NFL, a losing football player is worse than someone who doesn't play the game at all. We bad news birds used to sweat just as much as the then-champion Cowboys, but there were no parties for us, no parades, no cheers. There was only the personal satisfaction of doing our best. No one wants to hear about that.

The worst part of losing is what it does inside you. It eats at you and makes you sour. The only thing people want to know is why you're losing, and everyone figures there must be a simple concrete reason. Something your team did was wrong. Someone, somewhere, is to blame. What can I say? I never knew the answer, just the facts. Some teams lose.

When you lose, you don't expect anything either. Players know they are going to be ridiculed when they lose. Most NFL players never go to the Super Bowl, and they know because of it, they will soon be forgotten. As players on a losing team, we had to pay our way to Disney World. We knew you wouldn't buy our brand of soda or cereal or underwear. We weren't on the cover of any of your magazines. The fact is, with a record like ours, we really never blamed you.

WHY JERRY GLANVILLE
IS GOOD FOR FOOTBALL

When I first learned that Jerry Glanville was to be the head coach for the Atlanta Falcons I told my wife I would have to get traded. I had no intention of playing football for a guy who drove a Harley and wore a black hat. I always wanted to be a good guy. It seemed Glanville and his team in Houston, complete with their Dome of Pain, were nothing more than a band of criminals.

But, like so many things in life, Jerry Glanville was not what he appeared to be. Well, that's not entirely true. He was, and is, an outrageous personality who really does live his life in a way that most people consider to be crazy. The man you may have seen in dark glasses and a cowboy hat wearing a long duster and a belt buckle the size of a manhole is . . . well, eccentric. And that's the real Jerry. There is no show for the cameras here. The man is as funny and delightfully zany at the dinner table as he is doing an interview on national TV.

So, why is he good for football? Because of that personality. Jerry Glanville is like the taste of curry pepper when compared to many of the NFL coaching personalities, which are more reminiscent of overboiled noodles. He had two team buses during his reign in Atlanta, one for the guys who liked to fight, and one for the guys who didn't. He cited this rule to everyone who criticized his lack of team discipline and added further that, on the road, he insisted that no member of his team would be allowed to sleep with a dead woman or a live man. On weeknights, Glanville would do charity fund-raisers with the likes of Travis Tritt, Kris Kristofferson, Jerry Jeff Walker, and Confederate Railroad. He'd almost always join in onstage too, with his raspy Texas accent. Not bad for a kid from Detroit. During the off-season, we could always catch Jerry on TV, running the NASCAR circuit, crashing into walls and burning up engines.

One summer, after missing two weeks of training camp with a contract holdout, I returned to the team to learn that I and Jesse Tuggle, our middle linebacker and also a holdout, would be taking the team to a bar called Fat Tuesday's. For the remaining two weeks of camp, Jerry crooned about how we'd all go to Fat Tuesday's on the last day of camp, which was a Wednesday. I think he loved the play on words as much as the idea of making us take the entire team out on the town. The bill that night came to three thousand dollars, and I wish I'd had a camera to catch the look on Jerry's face when the manager brought him the bill all tallied up on his credit card, which I had pilphered from his office.

But Glanville was more than a jokester, a prankster, a race car driver, and a country-western singer. The man loved to coach football, he loved his football players, and he was singularly plugged in to the essential elements of the game. Glanville, although one of the most knowledgeable strategists in the game, understood that ultimately all the Xs and Os mean nothing.

He knew that football was a game of effort and sacrifice and intensity, of hitting and running and hustling and guts, and he had the ability to draw those qualities out of players that came from every imaginable walk of life.

I had more fun playing football for Jerry Glanville than I did since the days when we played in the backyard as kids, when the joy and love of the game was as pure as a perfectly thrown touchdown pass. When you won with Jerry Glanville, you bathed in it, you drank of it, you soaked your soul in the feeling of victory. His locker rooms and his sidelines were a hysterical mix of celebrities and music and singing and hand-slapping high fives. One year, after beating the 49ers with a last-second Hail Mary pass, one San Francisco player was quoted as saying, "Now I know what it feels like to be beaten by a circus." And he was right, they were beaten by a circus. They were a team of flogged galley slaves, quivering under the crack of a whip. The only consolation they ever had was the fact that they ground the rest of the league down with the same ferocity with which they were coached. But that year, it didn't work. The disciplined soldiers of the NFL had their beards pulled by the acrobats and the circus clowns.

It didn't last. For one reason or another, the team sagged back into its usual anemic condition. I like to think it wasn't Jerry though. I like to think that the unbridled joy of the game can survive the rigorous need to win at all costs. I like to think that as long as you give everything your heart has to give on the field all week long that off the field you can smile and have a laugh. I don't know though. Maybe you can't. Either way, a character like Glanville belongs in the NFL.

How TV Cameras and Microphones Change the Game

If you think that the players in an NFL game aren't only aware, but affected by the television cameras and microphones, you're wrong. The days when players played to the audience in the stands are long gone. Players often know when the cameras are on them whether they can see the little red lights or not, and they play to them as if they were on a Hollywood movie set. In science, the Heisenberg uncertainty principle says the nature of an object is changed just by the very fact that you are observing that object. Nowhere could that principle be more accurately applied than to football players, on the field, in the NFL.

Most players are avid football fans. If an NFL team isn't playing on Monday night, you can bet you'll find a large group of its players together somewhere in their home city watching the game. Even the Sunday night games on TNT and ESPN are avidly followed by players who can get to the TV set after their own game is finished in the afternoon. Part of being a fan of the game for players is being a fan of the broadcast itself. Players watch carefully what exactly it is that gets other players onto the screen, and when the network chooses to use a close-up and why. It's no coincidence that more and more players after scoring a touchdown, or making any big play, immediately whip their helmets off and come jogging slowly off the field, celebrating with teammates and inciting the crowd to make the biggest spectacle possible, while providing the television audience with a good shot of their helmet-less face.

The helmet is a real problem in the game of television and football. Players are savvy enough to know what face time means—recognition and increased opportunities for commercial endorsements—and many are eager to get as much as possible. This is why the helmets sometimes come off so quickly. It is also why players from time to time do outrageous dances or wear articles of clothing that have nothing to do with the team uniform. Players don't really wear bandannas to keep the sweat off their faces. They wear them to be different, to stand out and draw the cameras like a young lady changing in front of a curtainless window. The NFL has responded by penalizing and fining displays that are considered to be unsportsmanlike, and by levying thousand-dollar fines for sartorial infractions as well.

Players, though, are like convicts in a prison where cigarettes have been banned; somehow they find a way around it. Like the prisoners who roll up dried-out weeds in old gum wrappers, the players find a way around the rules. First it was Jim McMahon's headbands that were prohibited. No messages were allowed. Players started writing messages on the tape of their shoes. That got banned. Players wrote on their gloves, their elbow pads, their towels, any surface they could find. Now all writing has been outlawed. Everyone on a team has to have the same color gloves, the same color shoes, even the same three inches of white showing above the solid team color of the socks. But in their determination to draw the cameras, players came up with bandannas and multicolored Band-Aids. If those are prohibited, there will be something else.

When it comes to sound bites, you can never trust what you hear when a player has been "wired." Everyone in the league knows the story of Lawrence Taylor's sound extravaganza. Lauded by many as the greatest defensive player ever to take the field, his vocal outbursts were preserved on tape so posterity could know what it sounded like to line up across from LT. His teammates knew when LT was wired whether they'd seen the small transmitter and microphone being taped to his shoulder pads or not. Suddenly he was talking and bellowing and screaming like never before. This happens whenever anyone is miked during an NFL game. Players know it. They laugh.

Although players will consciously invent antics to ensure replays of their feats for days to come, we have to remember that they still have to deliver the goods in the first place. Neil Smith wouldn't be able to simulate knocking a baseball out of the park unless he first sacked the quarterback. Deion wouldn't be able to high-step into the end zone if he wasn't running back a kick or an interception for a touchdown.

Furthermore, if you cut these antics and fashion statements off your perception of the NFL (the same way you cut the mold off the surface of an exquisite cheese), what you've got is pure athletic magic. A spectacular run by Barry Sanders, for example, needs no trappings to be appreciated, or to stand out. A perfect pass by Steve Young and a catch by Jerry Rice needs no explanation. Troy Aikman pulling himself up off the ground, buckling his helmet back on, and setting his damaged chin with determination speaks for itself. And you don't even need to be a football fan to enjoy watching and listening to Ironhead Heyward blasting through defensive players like a discharged shotgun in a barroom brawl.

So although some of what you see and hear of NFL football can be unsightly if you are a purist, understand that there are people who like the pungent taste of mold, just as much as the cheese. They need that extra flash and pizzazz to give them something to talk about at the office or point out to their wife or girlfriend, something so obviously sensational that anyone will take notice and enjoy the spectacle just as they might enjoy watching a man juggling chain saws. And take comfort in the fact that beyond the inventive hoopla of made-up sights and sounds, there is never any deficiency of good hard-hitting in a game of NFL football.

Only an Ass
Would Kick a Zebra

To players in the NFL, the officials are nothing more than malfunctioning automatons. A zebra may go all day without making a mistake, but then, on that one inevitable controversial play, whichever guy had the call go against him is hating that zebra like a guy who ran off with his wife. When they do their job (which is the vast majority of the time) no one says thanks, no one even notices. It's only the gross errors or the close calls that generate interest from players, coaches, management, and fans alike. So, basically, these guys are the pariahs of the NFL.

They can't show too much personality on the field either. If they're nice to one player, the guy on the other side of the line would cry foul. When refs had pleasant things to say to me, which they occasionally did, it was under their breath, so no one else could hear. One thing I knew about refs, even before I stopped playing, was that a lot of them like to listen to National Public Radio. I had more refs throw compliments at me regarding my commentaries on NPR than I did flags for being offsides, which is saying something since I jumped the gun quite regularly. Don't get me wrong. They weren't all nice. Some of those officials, I swear, hated the world and everyone in it. They were mean, surly cusses, with mouths as foul as that of a drunken whore.

And if they had it in for you, it was trouble. Part of the reason the zebras are so reviled among players is that they're the judge, jury, and executioner all in one. If they think you grabbed a guy's face mask on purpose, you'll get that fifteen-yard flag and a blistering torrent of insults, even if the fact was that your fingers got caught between the metal bars and you were only trying to prevent them from being snapped off like toothpicks.

For an offensive player, practically the only time a ref throws a flag is if they did something wrong. The flag draws not only the penalty but the attention of the coaches to the error. For defensive players, penalties are usually judgment calls and right or wrong, there's no one for the player to appeal to if a ref makes a call that gets him ejected, fined, or marked as the goat who loses the game. That's a tough thing to take. That's why players will replay on game film over and over a zebra getting clobbered in the middle of a pile. Short of death, the more damage done to the official, the more mirthful the laughter of players and coaches witnessing the punishment.

It wasn't until I became a broadcaster that I really appreciated and understood NFL officials. I was amazed to learn not only of their human frailty but of the complexity and difficulty of their jobs. John Madden told me that a great broadcaster has to know the rules of football. That sounds easy, but it's not. It was when I set out to learn all the rules of the NFL, and their mind-bending exceptions, that I realized just how smart those refs have to be. As a defensive lineman, my knowledge of the rules of the game was minimal. If it moved, I hit it. That was about the extent of what I knew. While I was learning the rules of the NFL, really learning them, I was also studying for the New York State bar exam, which I was to take in the summer before my first season with FOX. I can say without question that after digging through the maze of words and concepts in the NFL rule book, even the most difficult areas of the law were nothing more than first-grade primers by comparison.

There are hundreds of exceptions to calls that are made on almost any given play when a penalty flag is thrown. When the zebras huddle together to confer with one another, they aren't arguing what did or didn't happen. That's already been determined. Like judges, certain officials have certain jurisdictions, and depending on their position on the field and their responsibility, only one of them will have the final say on any given call. What that huddle is all about is the seven of them going through the sequence of events and how those events affect the ruling they will make. For instance, if the ball is thrown on first and ten and tipped at the line of scrimmage, then caught by a receiver downfield where the receiver is then face-masked by the defense, what would the call be?

Most people would say it's simple. The penalty will be marked off to advance the offense either five or fifteen yards from the point the ball carrier was tackled. But if the ball was tipped at the line of scrimmage by an offensive lineman, the pass reception was illegal. The ball was dead when it hit the quarterback's own lineman. The ball comes back to the line of scrimmage. It is second and ten. If the official who called the face mask didn't know about the pass being illegal, then the wrong call could ensue. Thus, officials will huddle together to confer and make certain the exact sequence of events before they mark off any penalties.

No one in the NFL wants to make the right calls more than the officials themselves. Do they make mistakes? Yes, don't we all? The difference is that the zebras are not only chastised by players, coaches, and fans when they err, they are demoted by the league if their mistakes add up. Game tapes are sent back to the NFL offices every week and scrutinized. Only the officials with the best performances for the year get to do playoff games, and those who don't make the grade aren't asked back the following season. Just to get to the NFL, a ref must first have had at least ten years of college experience and endured three years of monitoring by the league before even being considered to officiate in the NFL.

I never realized how much pressure these guys are under until my first season as an announcer. I was flying back from a Green Bay Packer game and across the aisle from me was one of the game's officials. He was nervously gulping down scotch and sodas, listening to the crowd, most of whom had also been to the game, critique the game. I smiled and said hello to the ref and he leaned toward me with his eyes shifting about the cabin as though there might have been a rabid bat swooping about.

"Hey, how about that call when the quarterback ran for a touchdown?" he said.

"The one where it looked like he was out of bounds?" I replied.

He swallowed what I thought might have been a handful of three-penny nails before saying quietly, "Was he out?"

"Yeah," I nodded. "It was close. From one angle he looked in, but we got a replay on one camera where you could see he was clearly on the line."

"You sure, huh?" he said.

"Yeah," I said. "Why?"

"Oh," he gasped, looking straight ahead at the seat back in front of him like a man on his way to the chair, "that was my call."

"Well," I offered, "it really looked like he was in from one angle."

"But he wasn't," he said flatly.

"No," I said, shaking my head sadly.

The zebra looked down into his drink and sighed.

My perception of the officials had already changed. This was late in the season, and seeing them week after week before each game had softened me up considerably. I try to visit the officials' locker room before each game I broadcast to kind of bury the hatchet before I bury them on network TV for their bad calls. I apologize beforehand, reminding them that I've got people I work for too, and promising that I'll do my best to point out to the viewers when they do some of the really good things that they do. When I first started seeing these guys, milling around in a tight concrete bunker, somewhere in the bowels of the stadium, I couldn't help myself from thinking of Christians waiting for the show to begin at the Roman Colosseum in its heyday. They're a good bunch of people down there, with only themselves as friends. During Christmas week, one group told me, every group of officials visits an area children's hospital of the city where they're calling a game. They do it every year without fail, bringing NFL trinkets as gifts.

No one ever talks about that, or any of the good things the zebras do. The fans just throw cups of beer and everyone hurls insults at these guys as freely as vomit in a roadhouse bathroom. I think, though, that if people only knew how hard it is to do what these guys do, and if people realized these guys, unlike the players, aren't getting rich from being out there on Sunday afternoons, even though they risk their health and well-being almost as much as the players themselves, I think they'd give them a break. I'd love to see some of the windbags I hear kicking these guys around after a game try and do the same job half as well. They couldn't. It's too tough. Only an ass would kick a zebra.

Alternative Medicine
in the NFL

When people think of NFL players and medicine, they think of the latest medical techniques being applied vigorously to hardy and resilient physical specimens. Every person in Miami who has had his or her bones or tendons repaired by the same surgeon who repaired Dan Marino's Achilles' heel has bragged to at least one other person that they got the same treatment from the same doctor as one of the country's finest and most heralded athletes. People believe that if the magical medicine used to revive the tenants of the NFL can't help them, that they are beyond help. But when conventional medicine and surgery fail, people should take heart. Even the highly tuned athletic machines of the NFL have found relief in alternative sources of medicine.

Players from all across the league have turned to chiropractics, acupuncture, Rolfing, vitamins, holistic medicine, and even prayer, to cure the mandatory physical ills that accompany any NFL career. For the most part, these alternative sources of healing are not provided by the individual teams. In fact, there is an ongoing struggle between these increasingly popular forms of medicine and the old entrenched system of physicians and athletic trainers. Every team has a medical staff that includes one general practitioner, one orthopedic surgeon, one head athletic trainer, and several assistants. A trainer is somewhat akin to a physical therapist, although PTs and trainers alike would cringe at the comparison. The difference is that athletic trainers are specifically and practically trained to treat athletes, whereas PTs have a more extensive education in the sciences and, generally speaking, less of a specific focus on athletic injuries. As a rule, both groups think they are best suited to treat the injuries that arise from playing football. Athletic trainers, however, rule the confines of the NFL and most scoff at the notion of anything other than the traditional system of medicine.

Likewise, NFL physicians, like most physicians, consider anything but conventional medicine to be nothing more than dime-store magic tricks. To them, chiropractors, acupuncturists, Rolfers, and the rest are hucksters who simply couldn't make it into or through medical school. One NFL doctor explained to me that chiropractics was good for old people who needed some attention, someone to touch them and talk to them in a soothing voice. He believed that any real medical value of such treatment was exclusively psychological.

The NFL players, however, vehemently disagree. I've seen guys spend a lot of their own time and money seeking out and securing treatment from these alternative means. Chiropractors are so popular with NFL players that some teams have even relented and provided the players with access to spinal manipulation during the week of practice and even right before a game. For years with the Atlanta Falcons, the word "chiropractor" wasn't even allowed to be uttered. Then, when Jerry Glanville became coach, himself an avid seeker of chiropractic relief, we had a chiropractor available to us through the team. The chiropractor was not, however, allowed to perform his mystical crack- ings in the training room. Like a redheaded stepchild, he was given some closet or back corner in which to set up his unorthodox apparatus. Players and even some coaches would flock to him. As much as anything, I think most guys sought this kind of treatment because they were basically willing to try anything to get relief from their chronic pain and injuries.

For the same reason some players will get acupunc- ture, or try to heal themselves through meditation. Careers hang by tenuous filaments that are broken by inexplicably minute circumstances, leaving players to drop endlessly into the deep space that is life without football. If one player gets a vitamin injection before a game and he plays well, ten other guys will follow suit the next week. If another teammate gets Rolfed, an in- credibly painful massage therapy where fingertips are jammed into the connective tissue that lies between the bones and muscles of the body, and he caught three touchdown passes in the next game, you can bet every- one will want to get Rolfed.

Still other players believe in holistic medicine and prayer. They live their lives by certain credos, be it total biological intake or religious devotion, that they truly believe will help them cope with and heal their various wounds better than their unbelieving counterparts. Reggie White is of course the first name that comes to mind when you think of healing and prayer. During the 1994 season he damaged the ligaments in his elbow. Three weeks later on the day before a game that many people didn't expect him to play in, Reggie told me that God had healed his elbow. I have read also of players who are Christian Scientists who have attrib- uted healing to prayer. The thing that may surprise you is that there is more than just faith; there's scientific evidence to lend credence to what these guys are saying. Studies have been done that show people who are prayed for, even without knowing that others are praying for them, show a measurable difference in recovery when compared to individuals who are not prayed for.

Despite all the evidence of its effectiveness and the support that alternative medicines enjoy within the ranks of the NFL, most players look first to the doctors and trainers to get them well. Even the guys who do seek chiropractics, vitamins, and prayer to heal them turn to the doctors. Reggie White didn't shirk treatment from the Green Bay Packers' medical staff, and one of the Christian Scientist players I referred to didn't refuse reconstructive surgery either. The fact is, traditional medicine will never lose its place as the major source of treatment in the NFL. But, more and more, alternative methods of medicine are running a close second.

Preseason "Games": Why Waste Everyone's Time?

The NFL won't even call the four scrimmages each team plays during the month of August "exhibition games" or "scrimmages." To suggest more importance, they are titled "preseason games." However, to imply that these glorified practice sessions are anything more than that is a misuse of the word "game." It is a farce to dress the players up in the regular uniforms and parade them out in front of the football-starved fans in an attempt to pass the whole thing off as a game. It's like putting béarnaise sauce on chuck steak and calling it filet. In a game, both sides are usually trying to win. It matters. It counts in some way. But preseason scrimmages don't matter and they don't count. If they did, teams would be playing their best players in order to win. If the NFL really wanted to make these gatherings contests of any kind, they could require teams to play their predetermined squads by quarter, i.e., the first-string groups of both teams play the first twelve minutes. The other forty-eight minutes of the scrimmage would be split evenly between the second-string and third-string players giving them a chance to determine the final outcome. Obviously if one team's first-string seasoned veterans are going against another's third-string rookie free agents, the result is predetermined.

The one thing you will see in a preseason scrimmage is incredible feats of individual effort, especially from the second- and third-string players. These guys are holding on by their fingernails, struggling wildly to make an NFL team. They are haunted by the image of returning to their hometowns, cut and discarded before they ever even got going in the NFL, forever branded in their own minds as the guys who couldn't make it.

One of the most vicious hits I saw in a preseason scrimmage was by a rookie free agent who was probably slated to be cut the next week. But he was out there on the field in Green Bay when a drunken fan got loose and started running across the field during the scrimmage with security guards trailing close behind him. The drunk made the mistake of getting too close to this particular rookie and he threw a forearm at the guy's chest, laying him out neatly on the field without the guy getting the number of the bus that hit him. When the coaches saw that hit, and the player's complete disregard for human safety, that rookie had guaranteed himself a spot on the roster. These guys will battle like their lives are on the line. So, while you won't see the crisply executed plays of an aerial assault by Troy Aikman, you will see some of the best trench football going. This is another good reason to pit matching squads against each other and give the scrimmages some meaning.

Probably the most exciting facet of the preseason scrimmages is special teams. This is where the raw desire and insanity quotient of a new player can best be determined. Special teams requires more reckless abandon and heart than it does skill, so coaches carefully gauge how the younger players perform. Most younger players who make an NFL team will do so because they've done something impressive during the special teams plays of the preseason. If you watch this phase of a preseason game, and most people don't, you will see some of the best hits and most spectacular airborne feats of the NFL season.

For the established NFL veteran, preseason scrimmages are nothing more than an opportunity to get hurt. It is a status symbol among veteran players to not have to play in a preseason scrimmage. The ultimate compliment a team can pay to one of its stars is to not even dress him for a preseason scrimmage. The message is clear: You are too important for us to squander your talents and risk your well-being on a meaningless exercise. Coaches will play some stars on a limited basis, believing that they need to get into the groove of the real thing. But they should know that to NFL players who've been around, they would rather forgo that opportunity for the safety of the sideline. True competitors don't get very excited about a scrimmage that doesn't count. For the veterans who are thrown into the mix, you can expect them to perform out of fear, like tigers under the whip. They see that they are being used in a way that suggests they are expendable, and they fight hard to get back to the other side of the ledger. The problem is, the better the player, the more certain he is that what he does during these preseason scrimmages doesn't amount to a pocketful of bottle caps. If you're looking for the real contests with the best players brawling like it counts, you have to wait until September.

CONCUSSIONS:
EVERYBODY GETS THEM

Two seasons ago, concussions to quarterbacks Troy Aikman and Vinnie Testaverde and the retirement of Bears fullback Merril Hoge because of his head injuries prompted a spate of talk about the dangerous nature of football. Of course football is dangerous, and it's becoming more and more so. There are two reasons. First is the fact that so many games are played on artificial surfaces. I don't care what anyone's studies show or don't show. Only a fool would try to contend that these playing surfaces, which in most cases are nothing more than bright green living room rugs thrown over slabs of unforgiving concrete, are not markedly more dangerous than a field of grass. The second reason is basic physics: $F = MV$. That is, force is measured by multiplying mass by the velocity, or speed, of the object.

Let's look at it in real numbers. When I was a kid, it was a real big deal that the Steelers' Steel Curtain front four defenders had a total body weight of just over half a ton. That's about two hundred fifty pounds a man and that was big. Today, consider a guy like Big Daddy

Wilkinson of the Cincinnati Bengals. He's the proto-
type for the new age of defensive linemen. He weighs
three hundred twenty pounds and he's a lot faster than
the Steel Curtain guys ever were. He runs a 4.7 forty-
yard dash, a speed that is considered good for a linebacker or tight end in the NFL. It's the combination of
greater size and speed that together make football more
dangerous than ever.

You can't ask the players about this stuff, they're too
tough to admit what's going on. Troy Aikman is a
good example. During the 1994 season, Aikman took a
controversial and brutal hit from Arizona's Wilber
Marshall that many people decried as flagrant spear-
ing. That hit resulted in a concussion and multiple
stitches under Aikman's chin. The worst part about the
whole thing for Troy was his tongue. He bit right
through it on impact. He couldn't eat until midweek.
No big deal, he told me. Then, that very next week in
Cincinnati, he got hit on the same spot as he did the
week before by Marshall, right up under the chin, by
the crown of a Cincinnati linebacker's helmet. On the
replay, it looked like a Mike Tyson knockout punch.
"No problem," Troy told me. "Just part of the game."

This is a quarterback, mind you. These guys aren't
even supposed to be that tough. I know this concussion
routine myself. I can't even count how many I've had.
It's not that I've had more than a dozen, it's just that
it's something you don't think about as a player. It's
part of the game. There are different kinds of concussions; some are blackouts, some leave you dizzy, some
make you forget what has already happened in the
game. I've experienced at least one of each of these,
most players have, and most don't consider it anything
special.

Machismo aside, players will soon be forced to take
notice of their scrambled brains. Merril Hoge, for in-

stance, hung up the cleats after doctors told him he risked death if he got another concussion. In a TV interview after his decision, he had a hard time remembering the question he was asked only a minute before he started to answer it. With the intensity of the impacts on the rise and no end in sight, only the equipment can change to better protect the players. If the current concussion trend continues, look for the league to finally put some money into the research and design of a more protective helmet. Don't worry, owners won't foot that bill out of compassion for the injured players, but they will do it to protect their million-dollar investments. Already Dallas is using an advanced medical procedure to monitor the damage done to Aikman's brain. He will be getting a type of brain scan that will allow the Cowboys to see just how much damage he receives from future concussions. And, of course, he will get them. It's part of the game.

THE UNIFORM POLICE

When players take the field on Sunday, they know he's out there, somewhere, lurking, probably in the upper reaches of the stadium. He's there with his pen and his paper and his binoculars, probably dressed like an accountant in a tight-collared Brooks Brothers shirt. He doesn't need the rule book. He knows it by heart. And he knows exactly what he's looking for, things like an untucked jersey or the wrong color gloves. He is a member of the uniform police. He's making his list and checking it twice, and if you're naughty, he'll fine you five thousand dollars.

You might think that something as innocuous as a sweat towel would escape the long arm of the law, but to the uniform police, this is no laughing matter. If your towels don't conform to the NFL's *Policy Manual for Member Clubs*, Volume II, Rule 5, Section 3, Article 5C, which says, "such towels must be attached or tucked into the front waist of the pants and must be no longer than six by eight inches," then you can expect a fine sheet in your locker sometime during the next week. Although in fairness, I should note the flexi-

156

bility of this rule does allow that "a slightly larger size may be folded to these limits for wearing in games." How liberal.

It's not enough that NFL players have to worry about banging heads all afternoon with a guy like Nate Newton, the Dallas Cowboys' three hundred thirty-pound offensive road grader. What you've really got to worry about is your socks. That's right, because if you forget about Rule 5, Section 3, Article 3I, which says, among other things, that your sock must be a "one-piece stocking that includes solid white from the top of the shoe to no higher than the midpoint of the lower leg," it could cost you five large.

Now, I understand why the NFL has some of these uniform rules. Things were starting to get silly there for a while when Bears quarterback Jim McMahon used his headband as a billboard every week. (Although it was much better than using his bare ass as he did to a helicopter full of reporters at the New Orleans Super Bowl.) Football, after all, is not supposed to be professional wrestling, but these uniform police are tough. There's no due process in this sartorial legislation either. I had one teammate who was fined fifteen hundred dollars for failing to cover up the logo on a pair of unlicensed shoes. (The NFL, by the way, collects these licensing fees.) Never mind the fact that his misshapen feet demanded that he wear that special brand of footwear. There were more important issues at stake, like insuring that every player conform to Rule 5, Section 3, Article 4D. This requires "a small NFL shield logo on the front left groin area of pants midway between the fly opening and seam and 1/2 inch below the belt." NFL players certainly wouldn't want to forget who they are.

The Big Sellout

Like everything else, the game of football is changing with the times. The equipment has become more high-tech and the players, like engineers, doctors, and lawyers, are more and more specialized. Another sign of our times is where the games are played. It comes down to economics. Stadiums with lids can double as concert halls and convention sites. Fields with plastic grass are cheaper and easier to maintain. When my old team, the Atlanta Falcons, moved from an outdoor stadium to the Georgia Dome a few years ago, it tilted the balance between grass and artificial fields. Since then, two teams, the Patriots and the Chiefs, judiciously went back to grass and evened the score. But then the Rams moved from Anaheim to St. Louis and made it more likely than not that when you watch an NFL game it will be played on artificial turf. But to me, football is a game that was meant to be played outdoors and on the grass. Maybe I'm old-fashioned, or maybe it's just the kid in me that still thinks of a mud puddle or a snow squall as an adventure.

I can remember being ten years old and coming

home one dreary Saturday afternoon from a Little League football game. I was so covered with mud that my dad took me out back where he hosed me down on the lawn before we worked for a full fifteen minutes trying to peel the sod and clothes and equipment off my body. I'll never forget the feeling afterward of lowering myself into that steaming bath: I felt like a football player.

All our other sports are meant to be played in controlled environments. Hockey and basketball are played indoors. Baseball and tennis are wisely postponed if it even looks like rain. But football, the most primal and violent of our modern day American sports, was meant to be played in the elements. Sure everybody loves a clear fall day with a slight breeze and a temperature of about sixty-five degrees, but this is a sport where fighting the elements is just as essential as fighting your opponent.

If the Phoenix sun is so hot that you need an IV at halftime just to make it through the game, that's okay. If it snows so hard in Foxboro that the TV cameras can barely make out the players and a canny groundskeeper can plow the spot where a field goal will be kicked to win the game, that's okay. And if the rain is so hard in RFK Stadium that everyone's feet slosh in their shoes and players slide for twenty feet when they fall, that's okay too. Because clouds and fog and wind and grass and mud and rain and sun are all part of the game.

And grass is so much more honest than artificial turf. It's a cushion. It breaks your fall, and it tears before the ligaments in your ankles and knees do. And instead of turf burns that tear into your flesh like a hundred paper cuts, grass just stains your pants.

Sure it's nice for the crowd to stay warm and dry, but let them wear thermal socks and bring umbrellas, or thermoses of hot chocolate, or even flasks of brandy. Let them in on the fun too. And if they haven't had enough fluorescent light and stale, recirculated air all week at work, then let them stay home and watch on TV.

THE MOST VALUABLE
MAN IN THE NFL

When I tell you that a man by the name of Mike Woicik is the most valuable man in the NFL I first have to qualify that by saying that dollar for dollar he is. Woicik, although he does earn six figures a year from the Dallas Cowboys, is a man who makes less than even the lowliest free agent rookie player. And if you think this is just some sentimental piece about a guy who's a dear friend of mine, think again. In the summer of 1994, I took a limo ride with ex-Cowboys coach Jimmy Johnson. We were both newly hired members of the FOX Sports broadcast team and we were in L.A. doing some promotional work for the network. I was thrilled to be riding with one of the coaching legends of the game. I wanted to strike up an easy conversation. The only friend Jimmy and I had in common at the time was Mike Woicik, Jimmy's strength coach for the Cowboys and my good friend.

"If I ever do get back into coaching," Jimmy confided to me, "the first phone call I make after I get the job will be to Mike."

Jimmy and I both had a laugh on the rest of the football world, which failed to realize what we knew: An excellent strength coach is essential to winning in the NFL in the 1990s, and Mike Woicik is hands down the best there is.

I had the great opportunity to train under Mike during my four years as a player at Syracuse University. During that time, Mike turned me from a two-hundred-and-twenty-five-pound high school kid into a two-hundred-and-fifty-pound NFL first-round draft choice. My time in the forty-yard dash dropped from 4.85 to 4.58. That's how I ended up in the first round. My bench press went from 325 to 425. My squat went from 450 to 700. My vertical jump went from 27 inches to 34 inches. All these physical gains enabled me to get more quarterback sacks than anyone in NCAA history with the exception of Hugh Green from Pittsburgh. Woicik made it all happen for me. He made it happen for our team at Syracuse, then he made it happen for the Cowboys.

People used to think Mike was crazy. Gruff and grumbling, he had more in common with a Soviet scientist than an NFL weight coach. In fact, he used all the Soviets' latest training methods in making his football players the best they could be. He is zealous in his commitment to plyometrics training, a series of jumping exercises used to increase explosiveness. He connects his players to long lengths of surgical tubing and pulls them like shot in a sling to train their bodies to run faster than they originally knew how. All the while, Mike is, and always was, adamant in his stance against the use of any kind of performance drugs, most especially anabolic steroids. He's figured a way to make incredible physical gains without the use of the dangerous substances so many other weight coaches were pushing in the 1980s.

If you still don't believe me, or if you don't trust the

opinion of Jimmy Johnson, ask Jerry Jones how valuable Mike Woicik is. Even though I'm sure Jerry Jones would cringe to be on the same side of any issue with Jimmy, I know he'd vouch for the value of Mike Woicik. In 1994, Barry Switzer was contemplating firing Mike, since he was a leftover "Jimmy-guy." When word spread, Jerry Jones was implored by several big-name Cowboys players to keep Mike on the scene. One of those guys was Troy Aikman himself. Jones was so impressed with the outpouring of sentiment by the players that he re-signed Woicik to a new contract. Because football is and always will be a game of strength, speed, and explosiveness, that move was more important to the Cowboys organization than signing Deion Sanders. It was a hundred times cheaper too.

BLOODLUST

Blood is a beloved thing in the NFL. If a player can draw blood from another, it's like winning the big stuffed bear for your girlfriend at the fair. It means you've hit someone so hard that they burst. If a coach sees blood all over his players at the end of a game or a practice, he knows that some serious hitting has been going on and it warms his soul.

Equally important for a player is the disregard of one's own blood. I solidified my starting position for many years with the Atlanta Falcons by laughing at my own blood. During a scrimmage play in practice in the middle of a scrum, some hell-bent offensive lineman got his hand jammed up under my mask. One of his sausagelike fingers got slammed up into my nose and tore out enough flesh to leave it bleeding like a butchered chicken. The stun of the blow made me dizzy and I was fortunate that the next play called for a new defense of which I was not a part. I staggered to the back of where the offensive unit was huddling and mixed with the rest of the team as the trainers descended on me to try and stop the flow of blood.

Before they could get anything worthwhile going, the defense changed again. I was part of that next unit, but didn't know it because I was caught up in the attention of the trainers. When I heard Jerry Glanville, our coach, call my name, I started from the cluster of trainers and players gathered around to observe the gore.

"Coach," one of the trainers yelled, "he's got to get patched up."

"I'm okay," I said and jogged into the huddle.

Glanville turned to look at me. I looked like a casualty of war, not a football practice. The blood was streaming down my face, filling my mouth and spilling down my chin. I blew a crimson spray as I huffed and puffed from the exertion of the previous set of plays. Glanville's eyes narrowed. I looked like I'd taken a bullet in the face. Then he smiled. Don't get me wrong, but I think Jerry fell in love with me at that moment. There's nothing quite like the sight of blood to make a coach happy.

PLAYOFF BLUES

You might think that anyone who spent his NFL career with the Atlanta Falcons might not know the first thing about the playoffs. Well, you're not completely right. During my eight years, we Falcons did make a playoff appearance. We even won the wild card game in New Orleans in the 1991 season before getting swamped by the Redskins the next week in RFK. The 'Skins went on to win the whole thing, so we liked to make the argument that we were the second-best team in the league that season. Nonetheless, even I didn't trust my own experience in the playoffs enough to make broad statements about the sentiments it creates among NFL players. So I took the shocking results of my own team's emotions and compared them with a guy I know who played for that powerhouse of the 1990s, the Dallas Cowboys.

For us Falcons, the playoffs were a double-edged sword. You wouldn't think that, would you? I mean, after being starved for postseason play for more than a decade, you'd think we Falcons would have been in nirvana once we finally made it past Christmas. Well, we were thrilled, but that's not the whole story. The truth is, we weren't crying like babies when we lost that second playoff game in Washington. I hope wherever Jerry Glanville is when he reads this that he doesn't spit on my memory, but I'm only the messenger. The truth is, when you lose, you also win.

The playoffs, wonderful as they are, are an extension of a brutally hard season, a football season longer than any time in the history of the game. From mid-July until right around Christmas you run that body through the wringer. By December, you start feeling like a worn-out pair of jeans. Your knees start to wear away and you come apart at the seams. Mentally, physically, emotionally, your tank is on E. You roll into those playoffs on fumes, and when it's all finally over, well, win or lose, you're happy to shuffle off into the off-season and curl up in a corner somewhere to lick your wounds.

Now, I know exactly what you're thinking. You think that it is exactly this attitude, this lack of focus, of commitment, of perseverance that kept the Falcons out of the playoffs for a decade and hasn't allowed them to ever make a Super Bowl appearance. But you are dead wrong. This difficult and contradictory set of emotions happens to the players on every NFL team, even, oh yes, I'm going to say it because it's true, even with America's team, the beloved Cowboys.

The week before the 1993 Super Bowl I was in L.A., and I spoke to a guy who was a starting player for the Cowboys. I met him out one night and asked him the question that I knew no one else would. I asked him if they, the Cowboys, had the same despicable set of emotions about the playoffs that we lowly Falcons had had only two years before. I pointed out the length of the season, the pay cut most players had to take during the playoffs (the first round of the playoffs each man is paid ten thousand dollars for the week; it may sound like a lot, but most starting players regularly make more than sixty grand a week), and the joy with which every NFL player I ever knew entered into the off-season. When I told him how we felt, about not being all that sad when we were eliminated, he looked nervously around, as if someone might be listening. Then he leaned across the table and with a knowing smile told me this story:

"Last year we went to the championship game, and we lost. But we weren't sad. We were glad. When we were flying out to San Francisco, a buddy of mine leaned over to me on the airplane and whispered, 'You know, if we win, we win, but if we lose, we get to go home, so if we lose, we win too.'

"So, we lost the game, and on the way home we were drinking beer on the plane and my buddy raises his beer can and says, real quiet, so the coaches don't hear him, 'We lost, here's to the win.' Everyone toasted to that. We were glad as hell to have the season over with. The same thing happened this year. I mean, we wanted to win. We wanted to be here, but damn, it's almost February and we're still playing. That's like seven months of football. It's grueling."

Don't get me wrong. Not having played in a Super Bowl, let alone won, is the one thing about the NFL that I really regret never having done. It kind of separates the haves from the have-nots. And my confidant? That ring is something he'll cherish for the rest of his life. No one can take that world championship away from somebody who was part of it. The thought of that ring fuels a lot of fires in the hearts of football players of every age. So don't think of the playoff blues as a sign of the times, of players being selfish and only concerned with money, because that's not the case at all. In fact, don't make any judgments against anyone, not unless you played yourself. Even the NFL's coaches don't know that ground-up spit-out feeling of being a player, in January, in the NFL. And those guys raising their beer cans weren't disgruntled backup players either. They were the crème de la crème. Tough guys whose fortitude you wouldn't want to challenge. More than anything, the sentiments of players going into the postseason are a testament to just how unbelievably grueling an NFL season is on the guys who are out there, tearing up the turf.

Eating in the NFL

Of course most NFL players eat a lot. The question is what? And, is there any connection between what players eat and their success on the field? The answers are everything, and not at all.

There is no set diet in the NFL. Progressive nutrition would lead you to believe that these million-dollar athletes would be stoking their systems with just the right mixture of carbohydrates, proteins, and fats. The diets of NFL players, however, are as varied as the universities they hail from.

One thing you can place a safe bet on, except for some crazy kicker, you won't find any vegetarians in the NFL. The reason is simple: weight lifting. Almost every player in the NFL lifts weights extensively. That kind of exercise breaks down a tremendous amount of muscle tissue. That's what weight lifting is all about, breaking down the muscles so that they rebuild stronger than they were before. Part of that rebuilding is a high intake of protein. I'm not saying it couldn't be done. I am saying that to train with weights the way you need to in order to play in the NFL, you'd have to

170

spend half your day eating beans in order to get the amount of protein you needed to rebuild your muscles.

After the vegetarian angle, everything goes. Even pre-game meals are incredibly diverse. Not everybody is putting down simple carbohydrates at this meal, which is always served four hours before kickoff. Those car-bohydrates were exactly what I ate: spaghetti, French toast, two baked potatoes, and some fresh fruit, usually a banana and some cantaloupe. I thought I was pretty smart, using the latest knowledge to gain the edge on my opponents. But it didn't matter, I still had days where I was outrun and run over by guys who were packing away a breakfast of ham and eggs the morning of a game. I realized that eating was something as per-sonal as a lucky pair of socks.

Some guys to this day will eat a big steak four hours before game time. Those big bloody slabs of meat are lucky if they're gone from a guy's system by the next week's game. A lot of guys, myself included, wouldn't think of eating any kind of red meat for three days prior to a game. That steak routine is what they were doing back in the 1950s and 1960s, before the ideas of nutrition were very refined. Still, that old notion of an athlete getting strength from meat has died hard. The only way a team won't have some guys eating steaks before a game is to not have them available. Some teams have done just that. Halfway through my own career with the Falcons, they stopped serving steaks at the pregame meal. They replaced it with chicken, which also doesn't do a player one bit of good since it can't convert into the kind of energy he'll need by game time, but it does digest better than red meat.

The range of food is pretty broad. I knew one guy who wouldn't consume anything but carrot juice on the day of a game. I knew another who would slug down hot dogs and Coke at the stadium less than an hour before kickoff. I'd say the majority of players try to eat reasonably smart the day of the game and not too much since it would likely end up on the field or in the locker room sink. But during the week, you won't find many guys at all eating to win.

I think it's because football players tend to be visceral people that they enjoy eating and drinking as much as any group of people on the face of the earth. They like an ice-cold beer on a hot afternoon to wash down a fat grilled cheeseburger with everything on it. Who wouldn't? They like deep-fried seafood, sausage sandwiches loaded with peppers and onions, French fries, ribs, pizza, chicken wings, and mashed potatoes with gravy, followed by thick double-wedge pieces of pie backed up by planets of rich ice cream. Players love to eat all the things that everyone knows you shouldn't. They love it for the same reasons everyone does, it tastes great, and more because they can get away with it. Being an NFL player, you expend an incredible amount of energy. There are a number of players, I was one of these, who *have* to eat everything in sight if they are to have any hope of maintaining the size they have struggled so hard to obtain to become an NFL player. Even for the real heavyweights, food, and lots of it, is a way of life.

This is the same reason some players have weight problems after life in the NFL. They still have that eating habit that always lets them order dessert after dinner, but without the rigorous calorie-burning schedule of life in the NFL. For the guys who do keep their weight in check after their NFL careers, it's almost always because they somehow figure out a way to continue to vigorously exercise, not because they halted their see-food diets—seeing food, any food, and eating it.

COULD YOUR SON BE AN NFL PLAYER?

I hear it all the time now. I have two sons, ages six and two, and everyone is constantly asking me if they'll be football players. I tell people the kids should only do well in school and be doctors or something. But if they want to play football, I promise you I won't miss too many of their Little League games. Even though there are obviously many more important priorities in life for a young person before being a football player, I'd be lying if I said I wouldn't be proud if my kids played the game and played it well. All parents like to speculate on what their kids can and can't be. It's fun. It's okay. But none of us should forget that some kids, no matter how hard they work or how hard you push them, just physically cannot play football in the NFL. Just as some kids will never play in the NBA because they're not fast enough or tall enough, there are certain characteristics that will open the door for them to be great football players if they're willing to make the other inherent sacrifices.

One of the beauties of the game of football is that there are so many different types of players needed to make up a successful team. If your kid can't make it as an offensive tackle because he's not going to be six foot six inches tall and weigh around three hundred pounds, he might be able to make it as a kicker, if he's got a leg like a rocket. Don't think all kickers are flaky either. There are kickers in the NFL whom you could count on in a back-alley fight. The Bears' kicker, Kevin Butler, or Reggie Roby, Tampa Bay's punter, for instance. On the other hand, if your son shies away from contact and really minds getting a bloody nose, being a kicker is probably his only hope.

Besides kicking, the two essential physical elements necessary to play the game of football are size and speed. You have a lot of one or the other, or a good amount of both. For instance, your boy could be a veritable waif, five foot six and a hundred and sixty pounds, but if he can run a 4.2-second forty-yard dash, then he can learn to catch the ball and play wide receiver. If your son is going to be six foot eight and weigh three-fifty, he can gain the coordination and agility necessary to play on the offensive line and get away with being fairly slow. Notice, however, that even with the extreme natural abilities of size or speed, there is always an element of work that must be added in. Learning skills and training the body are essential for even the most physically talented football players.

So how do you get your kid to work? You don't. If a boy doesn't want to wear those uncomfortable uniforms, put up with the headaches, go through the grueling practices in the heat of the summer, lift weights year-round, put up with coaches bellowing at him and other boys trying to knock him off his feet, then there's nothing you can do about it. You can't make people play football, no matter how hard you try. Because to succeed at the game, you have to love it, or at worst, you have to be completely determined that you will stay with it no matter how bad things get, like the kid who works all summer cleaning bathrooms and putting up with it so he can afford to buy a car. Football gets like that, like cleaning bathrooms. Those practices and the physical training, day after day, are back-breaking, at times boring, and sometimes the whole thing really stinks.

Between the extremes of size and speed are linebackers, fullbacks, tight ends, and quarterbacks. With a few exceptions, these guys are all pretty fast and pretty big, but neither blazing nor enormous. It is in these positions that you can find an occasional mutt. By mutt, I mean not a purebred, a kid that really has no business being a linebacker or a tight end, because he's really not big enough, really not fast enough, but he's got that intangible that separates football from everything else. He's tough, tougher than a charred piece of chuck steak.

Still, even if your kid is that tough, there are limitations. I think a lot of parents should remember this. Nothing is worse than those fathers who think they can make up for their own shortcomings by pushing their kids mercilessly to excel in sports. Remember, NFL players are partly the product of hard work and determination, but the other half is pure genetics. So, unless you gave your kid that enormous size or those incredibly fast feet, lay off.

Finally, it's also important to remember when you talk about football and kids that every kid doesn't have to make it to the NFL to benefit from having played the game. I mentioned how hard and difficult it can be and that's true, but so is almost anything worth having. Sure, we've all heard about the teamwork and the physical exercise and the lessons on hard work. But football teaches one thing that kids can't get anywhere else. It teaches them how to get knocked down and get back up. It happens in football more than any other sport, and that's the only way you can really learn about getting back up. We all know that all our lives we're getting knocked down. It happens to the richest, smartest, and most famous people. The difference with a kid that plays football is that for the rest of his life he knows how to get back up. He knows from repetition that, hey, things happen, you get laid out. Football teaches kids to get up, over and over again, and that's why you see so many people in successful positions in life, not who played in the NFL, but who played football at some level as a kid and learned that lesson that stayed with them in everything else they did.

Why Some Teams Always Win and Others Always Lose

Imagine, if you will, a mansion, a one-hundred-and-fifty-million-dollar mansion. That's about the value of an NFL franchise these days. There are thirty of them around the country and essentially they serve up a feast of entertainment sixteen times a year on Sundays during the fall. The owners of these mansions do suffer. Everyone comes inside, they see the dirty laundry, they traipse mud in from the outside, they talk behind the owner's back, or worse, insult him to his face. But, as a consolation, the owners of these entities reap millions year after year, plucking it from the rest of us as easily as the feathers from a boiled goose.

We, on the other hand, expect to get a good meal. In football terms, we want to win. We want the playoffs. We want a Super Bowl. In some places, however, all you ever get is slop. Why? The answer isn't cut-and-dry, but it isn't voodoo magic either. Using the analogy of a mansion and a meal, I'll try to explain why it is that some teams always win and others always lose.

Essentially, there is one man responsible for a winning team. He is the owner. He has the control over the

177

house. He hires the cook, the butler, and every servant in between. If they all stink, whose fault is that? Their own? Who keeps them? Only the owner. The rest of us, walking in and sitting down, can only complain loudly. We can't send the cook packing, or the butler. We have no control over the menu or the quality of the ingredients. The owner, however, he can clean house. He can get rid of the cook at a moment's notice, toss the butler out on his tail, or open his purse strings and buy a U.S. grade A prime rib of beef.

In my analogy, let's think of the cook as an NFL coach. He puts the ingredients together for the meal. The butler is like a general manager, or the director of player personnel. This is the man who goes out and buys the ingredients, keeps the house in order, and oversees all the other support staff. The ingredients are like the players themselves, nothing more than life's staples like salt, flour, cinnamon, vegetables, and meat. These are obviously expendable commodities that can be bought and traded on the open market.

So what does this have to do with winning and losing football games? This simple domestic formula is exactly how they're won and lost. Owners, coaches, and GMs would like to have you believe that when the meal is awful, it's only a matter of some spoiled ingredients. They quickly assure everyone that the next meal and the next season will be much better. Players on the other hand would have you believe that it is the coaches, owners, and GMs who are responsible when they lose; the right ingredients were put together with the wrong recipe. Strangely, those same players gleefully stake their claim for exclusive credit when the team does win, as do those same coaches, owners, and GMs. You can't have it both ways guys.

Common sense tells us that, of course, if the meal is bad we don't blame the head of lettuce. We blame the head of the household. We don't chide the meat for being rancid or tough. Who gave us the meat? Who overcooked it? Who said it was okay to save money and buy flank steak instead of sirloin? Don't blame the players. But, if you think you've just died and gone to heaven because everything turns out so good, don't be daft and thank the noodles. It's the cook, the butler, and ultimately the owner who have given you your money's worth. It's no secret that you'll be back again, and tell your friends about it too.

So why talk about the three different men? Why not just say, hey, the owner serves up the meal? Because each of the three has a vital role in serving up a football season. A delicate balance exists among these men that can ruin everything if it's upset. Consider, for example, if the cook knows nothing about shopping, but thinks he does. If the owner lets the cook go along shopping with the butler and make the decisions for him, buying fish that's sat out too long, paying an outrageous price for strawberries that are out of season, and skimping on the wine to save money that was spent on bad strawberries, then the whole meal will be bad. You might look at the butler and spit on his shoes, but you'd be wrong. It was the cook who made the bad decisions on getting the ingredients and the owner who didn't have the smarts to tell the cook to mind the kitchen and let the butler do the shopping.

Also, it's very possible to have a good cook, and a good butler, and good ingredients, and still get a bad meal. Impossible, you say? Think about this:

Let's say the cook's specialty is Italian. He can make pasta and red sauce that makes your mouth water. Now let's say that the butler thinks the best thing for you is Chinese. He goes out and buys a lot of egg noodles and rice, soy sauce and shredded pork. The cook tries to use that stuff to make an Italian meal and it

stinks. Or the cook tries to make a Chinese meal because he knows the ingredients just aren't there for
Italian and it turns out badly anyway because he doesn't
know his chow mein from his egg foo-young.

This is exactly what happened with my team, the
Atlanta Falcons. Ken Harrock, the personnel director,
was buying ingredients for meatloaf, and Jerry Glanville,
the coach, was trying desperately to make a pizza.
Glanville almost pulled it off one year by making a
meatball pizza that got the Falcons and our fans to the
playoffs for the first time in a decade. I think Harrock
was so incensed at seeing his ground beef rolled into
little balls, instead of the glorious meatloaf he had envi-
sioned, that the next season he refused to keep any
yeast in the pantry and the pies went flat.

That kind of scenario happens all the time. Who can
stop it? Not the pepperoni. The owner, of course. He's
got to get a Chinese cook to go with his Chinese butler,
or an Italian butler to go with an Italian cook. Some
teams, like the Patriots, have Bill Parcells, who mixes
the ingredients, and also picks them. His butler goes
along to carry the bags, but Parcells calls the shots.
That's okay, obviously. There is a cook who knows
how to choose his ingredients well. The combination
isn't important.

Some teams, like the 49ers, have a complex hierar-
chy where everyone knows his job, stays within his
own territory, and does it well. At the top is owner
Eddie DiBartolo Jr. who knows enough to walk
through the kitchen, stick his finger in George Seifert's
soup, and give his opinion that it might need more salt.
DiBartolo would never just pick up the shaker and
start adding salt on his own. Some owners would do
that though, and they're the ones who always spoil the
soup. The worst situation is when one of the three entities, owner, GM, or coach, doesn't get along with the

other and doesn't want to cooperate to give us the winning team that we want. Again, it is exclusively up to the owner to recognize this and fix it.

This means one of two things. First, the owner must find a cook and a butler who are not only willing, but competent to work together. Or the owner must make it clear from the start that one or the other will be a subordinate. It's all about direction, having everyone in the organization working toward the same end and understanding what the final menu will be. If it sounds simple, it's because it is. It's so simple that it's hard to understand why some teams always win and others always lose.

LUCK AND THE DOGHOUSE

You'd think one of the nice things about playing in the NFL is that your job performance could be objectively appraised. To a certain extent this is true. You either complete the pass or you don't, catch the ball or drop it, make the block or get knocked backward, tackle the runner or get run over. These things can be seen and measured. Sixteen quarterback sacks in a season earns you a trip to the Pro Bowl. Quarterbacks can now be rated by a complex mathematical formula that quantifies their effectiveness. Players win starting jobs and become stars based on hard numbers like these.

However, the subjectivity that plagues most workplaces, determining who gets passed by for promotion and who skyrockets to the top of the ladder, is also a very real part of the NFL. Despite all the numbers that measure success and failure, careers can be made with a little luck, or destroyed by getting into a coach's doghouse.

Think about Steve Young. When he came to the NFL from the defunct USFL he was picked up by Tampa Bay. He floundered along with everyone else there, and was considered a failure. He didn't have what it took to be a star in the NFL. A lot of people were certain of that. Then he went to San Francisco. After playing behind Joe Montana for years, Steve Young finally got his chance. But, despite performing on an equal or better than equal level with Montana, Young was proclaimed something less than a superstar. The 49ers lost in the 1993 playoffs to the Cowboys and the following season were defeated in a head-to-head meeting with Montana and his new team, the Kansas City Chiefs. San Francisco was struggling.

But, if you remember, the problem with the 49ers was their defense more than anything. They were getting hurt in the passing game. Enter the league's best cornerback, Deion Sanders. Suddenly, the 49ers' defense was one of the best. Young just kept doing what he was doing, and the team went on to win the Super Bowl, making Steve Young the toast of the entire country and prompting people to finally declare his unadulterated stardom. Tampa Bay? Wrong place, wrong time. San Francisco? Right place, right time. The difference? Obscurity and stardom. This is not to denigrate Steve Young's accomplishments. He was the same great quarterback when he was with Tampa Bay, only no one could ever know it. This is part of the reason why Steve Young has such a level head. He knows what it feels like to be at the bottom, and if you talk to him, he'll be the first one to tell you that he got lucky.

Same thing can happen the other way around. Some guys never get lucky at all. Ever hear of an offensive lineman named Rich Moran? Didn't think so. Moran was one of the meanest nastiest run-blocking guards in the game of football. So why don't you know it? Because he played an obscure position for the Packers from 1985 until 1993, one of the team's longest playoff dry spells. Had this guy played for the Redskins during the same time, he'd have been one of the infamous Hogs. Believe me, this guy would have fit right in. People would have noticed and remembered him. He would have gone to the Pro Bowl time and time again. But he didn't. Bad luck.

One way to ensure that luck will never find you is by getting into a coach's doghouse. Of course not everyone can get into the doghouse; some players are immune, just like the boss's nephew at the office. The big-name guys don't have to laugh at the coach's jokes or send cards at Christmas. I've seen guys with multi-million-dollar contracts actually sneer in a coach's face. But the average player, you better believe, is just like everyone else. When Jerry Glanville showed up in Atlanta dressed like a Texas Ranger, all of a sudden the whole team started wearing cowboy boots. The guys who were really uncertain about their jobs even started wearing big silver belt buckles. If you're just one of the pack, and the coach doesn't like you, the mistakes you make will be noticed a little more, and the good plays you make will be passed off as feats that anyone in your place could have accomplished.

Inside the objective game of wins and losses, and tackles and interceptions is a kind of gymnastics meet, where every day, in practice and in the games, a football player is being judged by the coaching staff for his effort and performance. While certain remarkable feats earn anyone a ten, the majority of a player's career is made up of relatively inconsequential plays where his success is a matter of complete subjectivity. And so, just like in the office, the guy who is liked by the boss finds himself getting the better opportunities to succeed. He gets to run the stunts in the pass rush, making his chances better for a quarterback sack. He gets the ball thrown to him on an important play, solidifying him in everyone's mind as a clutch player. On the same play, the guy in the doghouse may have run a perfect pattern and gotten wide open. He may have been able to make the big catch and score a touchdown, but he never got the chance. Instead of giving him a high mark for his perfect pattern, the doghouse guy will be chided for not making a better block on the cornerback after the catch.

So the next time you're daydreaming on your drive home from your job about how nice it would be to work in a place that measured everyone on an equal and objective footing, don't make the mistake of thinking that that place is the NFL.

Why Steve Young Is a Better Quarterback Than Joe Montana

It is not uncommon for people to mistake Joe Montana's status as the most famous quarterback to ever play the game of football with his also being the best quarterback to ever play the game. One of the greatest, he no doubt is. But the man who many felt was nothing more than a pretender to Joe Montana, Steve Young, is not only the real thing, he's one better. Like many great success stories throughout history, Joe Montana was at the right place at the right time. Whether or not Steve Young will benefit from those same generous circumstances remains to be seen, but it is doubtful.

When Eddie DiBartolo Jr. finally got the 49ers on track in the early 1980s, Joe just happened to be there. Out of college he wasn't chosen until the third round despite being a star and a game-saving quarterback at Notre Dame. The reason more than anything was Joe's arm. It was reputed to be less than the rocket launcher big-time NFL quarterbacks are supposed to possess. But timing is everything. Joe fit into Bill Walsh's system perfectly. The big long ball wasn't as necessary as the well-timed underneath pass that Walsh used to surgically move his offense down the field in a way that was then new to the NFL. Joe grew with this system through the 1980s and it became second nature to him. He won four Super Bowls. He also had Walsh at the helm, incredible receivers to throw to, a solid and viciously dirty offensive line to protect him, and a running game to keep opposing defenses on their heels.

Under the old rules, when free agency was just a dream, teams like the 49ers could put together great teams and sit comfortably with their personnel for years. Players couldn't pick up and go the way they do now. Montana benefitted from this by working as part of a machine whose parts were well-oiled and dependable. It most likely won't happen again like that in the history of the game. Now when teams win the Super Bowl or go to the playoffs, the other teams who didn't, think that the players on the teams who did are better than their own. So naturally, if erroneously, they jump on these players from winning teams in the off-season, luring them away from teams like the Cowboys and the 49ers with premium prices that they are now forced to pay because the collective bargaining agreement makes even the cheapest teams like Cincinnati and Pittsburgh spend a certain amount of their millions on players' salaries. The players that go rarely help the teams they go to, but they weaken the teams they've left quite nicely. Chemistry and balance is a crucial part of the winning formula.

Steve Young will likely never have the stability of team chemistry that Montana had year after year, so he may not be remembered by the people who don't know football as a better quarterback than Joe. He may not win four Super Bowls. But he'll still be the better of the two. The reason is simple. He can run.

Both Montana and Young had and have an excellent grasp of a complex and highly successful offensive system. Both quarterbacks have accurate arms, mobility in the pocket, and impeccable timing. Montana wasn't even a bad runner, but he's nothing compared to Steve Young.

Young is as good as Joe ever was in his accuracy and his elusiveness in the pocket when it comes to avoiding pass defenders who break through the line protection. But Steve Young in the open field is as nifty a runner as Randall Cunningham, only he's more durable than Cunningham, and a much better passer. Also, Young along with Troy Aikman and Brett Favre are the toughest quarterbacks in the NFL to knock out of a game. They're like those weighted punching clowns you see little kids playing with. You can punch them, knock them over, stomp on them, or poke their eyes, and they just bounce right back at you. Steve Young is probably the only quarterback in the league since Terry Bradshaw who could just as easily have had a career as a running back. Besides running, his arm is strong enough to throw a long ball that's much closer to what Dan Marino can do than Joe Montana ever dreamed of.

When we used to play the 49ers and Young was Montana's backup, we were given an edict never to hurt Joe Montana. "Bring him down, but never knock him out," head coach Jerry Glanville would say. Although the 49ers usually trounced us anyway, we knew that if Steve Young was back there at quarterback, we didn't stand a chance. One game, when Montana was already out because of an injury, we had to face Steve Young. Thankfully, we knocked Steve Young out of the game, and, yes, we won.

Except for knocking him out of the game there really is no way to defend against Steve Young. If you try to blitz him, you most likely waste your linebackers because even if they can get through the line and get to him, they can rarely take him down. He's as slippery as they come, and if he breaks the pocket, he's just as dangerous running around the field as he is when he stands back in the pocket, unmolested, looking for a receiver. On the other hand, if you give him time, he'll stand patiently back in the pocket until he finds an open receiver. You're damned if you do, damned if you don't. Because he can run like Barry Sanders and pass like Dan Marino, he's the single most dangerous player in the game right now, probably ever. If that isn't enough, for those who think winning Super Bowls is the only measure of a great player, which they're not, he's now done that too. So, if you ever hear someone saying that Montana is a better quarterback than Steve Young, you know right away that he doesn't know football.

WHY PLAYERS CAN'T JUST WALK AWAY

We've all heard the horror stories of ex–Super Bowl champions run on hard times who pawn their big gaudy diamond rings so they can have money to pay the rent and get their next meal. Occasionally a newspaper story will appear chronicling the story of how some ex-NFL player ends up on the streets, homeless, when only recently he was in the penthouse of life. Most people have heard about John Riggins, the Redskins' superstar fullback and Super Bowl MVP who struggled with alcohol and was last reported to be living in a trailer in the backwoods of Maryland. The stories of fallen stars are countless. The question is, why?

It is the rule, not the exception for a professional football player to be dragged from the field by the heels with his fingers raking deep in the turf like lock-jointed hooks. Sometimes they pretend they're walking away, to save their pride, but it's really not their choice. Even the big stars don't just "retire." They're called sometime during the off-season upstairs to the team offices where it is explained to them that they have outlived their usefulness or become too much of a financial burden to justify any longer. But NFL players don't want to leave. It's not just the money either, although that's certainly part of it. Football players are spoiled with attention and special treatment and are never anxious to take their place in the real world.

It begins early on. Any player who ultimately makes it to the NFL is a star in his younger days. They are the favorite sons, almost without exception. Mom gives them extra money to go to the movies on Saturday night, or to buy that expensive pair of sneakers that they feel they really need. Little brothers and sisters and their friends gaze on with starry eyes as these football players waltz through life, with adults fawning over them because they can run or throw or hit better and harder than the rest of the kids. While the rest of his classmates are struggling to impress college admissions people to get into schools of their choice, the football player is being wined and dined by colleges across the country. He meets with powerful alumni, university presidents, and even noted professors, all successful adults who implore him to join them in their quest for a bowl game or a national championship.

When he gets to college, a football player finds that everything is taken care of for him. There is no rent, no bills to pay, or loans to worry about. Food is prepared and laid out at training tables without a word of appreciation expected in return. Tutors are available, free of charge, and professors are expected to understand that exam schedules have to be altered at times to accommodate team travel. Easy classes that keep a player's head just above the eligibility level are all mapped out. There is usually at least one person to monitor every player's eligibility status at all times. Summer jobs are a given. Again, the cream of the crop, the ones who will one day become NFL players, are given the best jobs. That means ten, fifteen, eighteen dollars an hour with little or no responsibilities. You won't find top-notch players scrubbing floors and toilets.

Then he arrives. The NFL rolls out the red carpet pasted with hundred-dollar bills. Training camp is brutal. The physical demands are incredible. But these are things that by now the player has become used to. He has played this game, maybe not as fiercely or as hard, but he has played it all his life. And now, the big checks start rolling in. I've seen players' paychecks for two weeks be in the hundreds of thousands of dollars. How do you think that feels? The first time a football player is really out on his own in the world, he's got a credit card with a fifty-thousand-dollar limit and maybe a million dollars in the bank, maybe much more. Despite this incredible wealth, some players don't know how to make airline reservations, get a mortgage, open a checking account, or do their taxes. But it doesn't matter now anyway, because he has so much money that he can easily find someone to do it for him.

And that's how most players go through their NFL careers, with other people doing everything for them. It costs them. It costs them dearly. But they have so much money, and they really don't see the end in sight. They don't know any better. For most guys there never was a time when someone wasn't taking care of their real-life necessities. As long as they scored the touchdowns, made the tackles, caught the passes, someone else took care of where they slept, what they ate, and paying the bills for living. I'm not suggesting that players don't earn it. They do. They endure things that few other people could. It's just that when they're no longer useful to the game, the ease of living comes to a tumbling halt.

Some players are able to convert the energy that made

them successful on the field into business acumen that propels them to inordinate success in the outside world. But for many guys, the emotional transition is too bewildering. Money dries up quickly. Parasitic "friends" move on to other hosts. Bankers no longer smile when they walk through the door. Credit card companies no longer understand. Car dealers want money up front. People expect them to get their hands dirty, step in line, quiet down, say please, be thrifty, exercise caution, and show remorse, all things that are now like some forgotten language they learned in early childhood, but were never really proficient in. Meanwhile, a player looks around and sees his nonplaying peers, guys who only wanted to buy him a beer in college and get close so they could say they knew him. They have established lives. They're entering the mid-level executive ranks, or they own thriving businesses. They know how to get along in the world. But the player? It's time for him to start from scratch. And these old acquaintances? A player is lucky to get a job in the mailroom from these guys. They don't want to be his chum anymore, because the party is over. That's why no one wants to leave. That's why it is a rare thing to see an NFL player walk away.

AGENTS: THE GOOD, THE BAD, THE UGLY

Agents are people too. Many football players don't believe that. Many look upon agents as a member of the rodent family. Agents can be that, but they can also be a blessing to football players who know nothing of the real world and are in desperate need of someone to counsel them. Players are coached all their lives in almost everything. They naturally seek the advice of people around them like kids in a kindergarten class. And like kindergarteners, they have no real experience with the slick characters of the world when it comes to assessing truth and veracity. They are ready to trust their agents. In a word, they are suckers. Sadly, many agents abuse this same trust to bilk their clients out of thousands, even millions, of dollars.

There is really no regulation of football agents. The NFL Players Association does what it can by certifying agents after they have gone through its education and training program, but there is no law requiring players to use certified agents. The NFLPA does, however, make a presentation to college football players at the pro combines imploring them to use only NFLPA-certified agents. There is no requirement either that an agent be an attorney, although many of them are. Typically, agents take 3 to 5 percent of a player's contract and get an additional 10 to 20 percent of any endorsement deals they broker. Some players have lawyers who specialize in contracts negotiate their deals, paying them an hourly rate. A few players use family friends or even their fathers to negotiate their contracts with teams.

The fact is, the value of a player's first NFL contract is mostly predetermined by the spot that player is chosen in the draft. Give or take the unusual exception, players will generally get a little less money than the player chosen in front of them and a little more than the player chosen behind them. It doesn't take great skill to determine the fair value of a player's initial contract. Despite the lack of skill and expertise required, an agent who hits the jackpot with a high first-round draft pick may be looking forward to getting paid 5 percent of one or two million dollars a year (fifty to a hundred thousand dollars a year) over four years for a negotiation that may take less than a week. It's good money, and when players see the ease with which these contracts are negotiated, they usually resent it.

To placate their clients, most agents will offer "full-service" representation, which means they will serve as financial advisor, marketing consultant, accountant, and glorified baby-sitter for their players. Thousands of players through the years have watched their money disappear because they've allowed their agents to manage it for them. The "full service" turns into self-service for the agent, who now has easy access to the player's money. The majority of agents are not qualified to provide anything but the most rudimentary advice regarding an investment portfolio. But it's easy for someone to palm himself off as an expert in this area to someone who has never held more than a hundred dollars in his hand at one time. It is not unusual for the agent to purchase life insurance annuities, bond funds, and other investment products on behalf of a player and receive kickbacks or perks from the financial or insurance agent selling the product.

I myself was convinced to put three hundred and fifty thousand of my five-hundred-thousand-dollar signing bonus into an insurance annuity that was an investment appropriate for a forty-year-old businessman. The commission someone earned on my mistake was somewhere around thirty-five thousand dollars. Ultimately, when I found a competent and independent financial consultant, I removed my money from that annuity at a substantial penalty, to reinvest it in more appropriate and higher-yielding vehicles. And I was supposed to be smart.

Maybe I was smart. More likely, I was just lucky. I never went into any of one of my agent's limited partnerships. Many of my counterparts, including a college teammate who recommended this agent to me, were bilked out of hundreds of thousands of their hard-earned dollars when those limited partnerships dried up. They were development and building renovation deals where the agent had easy access to the cash supply. He spent it. That agent, who was an attorney, was eventually sued and ultimately disbarred, but the players never recovered much of the money they had lost.

When it comes to marketing a player, agents promise the world, but typically deliver nothing more than a stale sandwich. When they first come into your life, NFL agents are a slick lot. Even the good ones have to be able to sell themselves with the cunning of a used-car salesman. There are so many agents out there scrambling for a chance at this easy money that the competition is fierce. Agents will promise everything from having the ability to move a player higher up in the draft, to securing valuable endorsement deals during a player's career. No agent, however, has ever done anything to have a positive effect on a player's selection spot in the draft. If anything, an agent with a bad negotiating reputation can make teams shy away from picking a player. And when it comes to endorsement dollars, agents sit back and cash in only if the player hits it big. The vast majority of NFL players don't have big endorsement opportunities. A few thousand dollars here or there to hawk mattress sales or card signings on local TV and radio aren't uncommon, but the six- and seven-figure deals are there only for the big-name players, the superstars. Agents have nothing to do with a player's ascension to stardom, but if a player does make that ascent, the agent will be right there beside him, fielding the endorsement requests coming in and taking his cut.

Of course agents use every imaginable inducement to get players to sign on the dotted line. From drugs to prostitutes, to vacations, cars, and envelopes of cash, some agents will give whatever it takes. When the player's contract is ultimately signed, the agent of course deducts the cost of these predraft perks directly from the player's signing bonus. What appear to be lavish gifts of friendship turn out to be merely unsecured loans for vices and luxuries. But despite the availability of these "promotional items," most players simply want an agent they can trust. The problem is, how to find one.

Agents wear many different disguises. The Good Christian talks about his faith and honesty and praises God to buy a player's confidence before he robs him blind. The Righteous Brother talks the ghetto talk and sucks the player into thinking that they have a common bond. They do—the player's bank account. The High Roller pulls wads of hundred-dollar bills out of his

pockets and always has some good snort in his breast
pocket. He gets a cut of his players' money in their
contracts and their drug deals. Then of course there is
the Wolf in Sheep's Clothing. This guy looks like an accountant, and he steals like a successful white-collar
criminal.

Many players choose their agents by word of mouth,
relying on past teammates to recommend their own
agent and vouching for his veracity. Despite what
seems to be a pretty safe way of choosing an agent,
players get taken anyway. The recommending client
sometimes doesn't even know he's being bilked, or the
new guy may not turn out to be as big a prospect and
thus get ten times less attention than the guy who was
vouching for the agent's care and concern. I witnessed
two teammates during my career have almost all the
money they earned bilked from them by an agent who
had them buy rental properties. What he didn't tell
them was that he was buying these properties himself a
few months ahead of time, then turning around and
selling them to the players at a hefty profit. When there
was a glut in the rental market and the properties
couldn't cover the mortgage payments, the banks came
in and demanded the difference from the players. These
guys lost hundreds of thousands of dollars.

The same agent had the gall to woo one of these guys'
teammates in the middle of all this chicanery. The players who were bilked warned the new guy that the agent
was a dishonest snake who had essentially robbed them.
I don't have to tell you that the new guy signed with
the agent anyway, do I? Successful agents, more than
anything, have the ability to sell themselves to football
players. Despite the appearance of past wrongs they
have committed, or things they have said, a good agent
can convince a new player he is not only a competent
negotiator, investor, and marketing maven, but a true,

down-home friend. That's how they do it. They sell themselves as friends.

In the midst of all this sleaze and slime are many attorneys who love to represent players simply to be close to the world of sports. They are honest characters who do their best to hold a player's hand when things are going bad, and step back out of the spotlight when things are going good. They give sound money advice. They attempt to get the player to live under the constraints of a budget. They come up with a financial plan that will carry them well into the future. They encourage their continuing education or job experience in the off-season. These are the guys you usually don't hear about, and they are the exceptions because they are extremely vulnerable to losing clients to the fast-talking snake oil salesmen who promise players more of everything if they'll only make a change. To compete in this world is a difficult thing for a decent self-respecting attorney, because it takes too much time and effort to seduce young players to become clients. The vast majority of "work" an agent does is just getting the clients. Once they have them, it's not too hard to play them like puppets and either advance their financial cause, or skim just a little bit more off the top.

WHY PLAYERS LOSE
THEIR MONEY

Most of the time, that is exactly what happens. Players lose their money. Everyone wonders how. It's easy. Players don't realize that money is one hundred times easier to lose than it is to make. When you're trying to make money, nobody is usually helping you. But when you want to spend money, everybody has got an idea on how they can help you. The problem with players is, they get too much too fast to realize how quickly it goes once they stop playing ball. By then it's too late. Either the well is already dry, or the player is too used to going to the well too often. They are similar to lottery winners in the respect that they acquire a large amount of money fast without having had the time to grow accustomed to it or without having been raised in an environment that would help them understand how to hang on to it.

What also happens is that players get greedy. They work all their lives to attain the prestigious wealth that is inherent with playing in the NFL. When they finally get that big payoff, players want to double their money overnight. Everyone has heard the adage that it takes money to make money, and many players mistake this idea with the certainty that people who throw a hundred thousand dollars into an investment will double it within a year. Players think the more money you invest, the bigger your return will be. No one who's trying to get them to invest talks to them about risk. People come out of the woodwork with limited partnerships, franchises, overly optimistic spreadsheets, and scams, promising the naive player great returns on his investment.

Besides being conned by their agents, players probably lose the most money to their family and friends. Brothers have great ideas for nightclubs, fathers are ready to open construction companies, mothers need new homes, cars, and vacations, and friends are excited to get going on every get-rich-scheme imaginable. It is because players trust these people so much that they so willingly fork over their hard-earned dollars. Of course these ventures all go bust. The people, the family and friends, never have the requisite business experience to make these things work. How many players have opened restaurants? I can't even count. Restaurants and nightclubs are just the kind of business that everyone thinks he can succeed in. But those businesses are harder than almost any other because of the dreadful hours, the stiff competition, and the cash that gets easily misplaced in the employees' pockets without anyone knowing.

People are shameless when it comes to asking athletes to invest money in their harebrained schemes. The average person thinks that every NFL player has more money than he can ever spend. The better the friend, it seems, the more insistent he'll be that the player must give him what he believes is merely the seed money to attain his God-given right to untold wealth. Players quickly become the desirable catalyst for everyone

around them's American dream. When I was a player I
had offers to invest in everything from trailer parks to
dairy farms and driving ranges. I watched guys lose
money investing in everything from real estate (probably the number one killer of NFL bank accounts) to
doughnut franchises and from candy machines to pyra-
mid scams.

And believe me, even if they don't lose money in
bad investments, it doesn't take long for most guys
to spend it. I've watched teammates with annual
million-dollar contracts, who never lived in anything
better than a run-down apartment until they came to
the NFL, instantly acquire champagne tastes that
kept them living from paycheck to paycheck. It is a
rare occasion indeed for an NFL player to save his
paychecks as if each one could be his last, which is
exactly what they could be. Most players are overly
optimistic about their careers and their future earning potential. Everyone thinks they will be the next
superstar to sign a million-dollar deal, and a lot of
guys live that way before they even see that kind of
money.

Even for the guys who don't acquire the financially
fatal habits of drugs or gambling, which some do,
they find ways to outspend their income. The biggest
liability players seem to find themselves with is a big
house with a big mortgage whose payments quickly
eat up what savings they might have once their career
is over. When it's all over a player is lucky to make in
the neighborhood of thirty thousand dollars a year,
the same money most NFL players make in a week.
It's pretty hard for players to adjust their tastes
downward. Living in a duplex and driving a Ford
Escort somehow has no luster after a guy has spent
years wheeling up to a mansion in a Mercedes con-
vertible. Yet most ex-NFL players I knew ended up

adjusting downward in the home market and driving economy cars relatively soon after the ends of their careers. One teammate of mine would buy a new car almost every month, trading in the BMW for a Porsche, then the Porsche for a Mercedes, then back to another BMW model, over and over, losing ten to fifteen thousand dollars on each transaction. How long do you think that can go on once his career is over?

In an attempt to help his client avoid these kinds of pitfalls, one agent I knew set up an NFL player's contract to pay him an annuity of about two hundred thousand dollars a year for life. It was a foolproof way to keep that guy from outspending his income and set him up for a life of ease. But the player did what looked to be impossible. He probably never imagined it could happen, but creditors attached that annuity and quickly lined up in front of him to collect the payouts. Anytime there is a supply of money, a valid creditor can get to it before the debt-ridden owner or beneficiary. There is no such thing as a foolproof way to keep a player and his money together. This particular guy decided to go into business with some other people. They did everything first-class, big offices, fancy restaurants for potential clients, the works. When it all went belly-up, someone had to pay the bill. The player's partners didn't have two nickels to their names, but he had his annuity.

Basically, it comes down to a total lack of sophistication. Most NFL players are just that, football players. They don't have advanced educations in law or finance, and they don't have the business experience to survive in the world outside football. They think that because they are big and tough, that no one would dare to rip them off. They don't know that the real world can be more cruel and more treacherous than even the football field. The adage is true more times than not: A football player and his money are soon parted.

In the Locker Room
Before, During, and
After a Game

BEFORE

During the ten minutes before a football game, the anxiety is so incredible that I used to wonder what made people ever want to play the game. Other players share this emotion. If you aren't sick with worry about the impending contest, then you don't care about winning, and if you don't care about winning, you don't wind up playing in the NFL.

During a Saturday prebroadcast interview with Chris Spielman, the Detroit All-Pro linebacker, my compatriots at FOX were astounded when Spielman bleakly described the torturous emotions of a football season.

"You know," he said, looking at me with a conspiratorial eye, "it's no fun. It's miserable. Until you get on the field and play the game, the week is murder. I don't sleep too well."

I did know. I knew exactly what he was talking about. The pressure to perform well, the pressure to win, the pressure to defeat someone across from you, haunts your every moment during the football season.

These tensions mount in a crescendo that reaches sickening proportions just minutes before kickoff. Now is no time for heroic speeches. Those are make-believe. Now is the time to purge the bile by vomiting into a pail. This is where the movie image of a player banging his head against a locker comes from. Moments before it's time to go out on the field, the locker room is a mob of jiggling, shaking, cursing, growling men. Their eyes roll like crazed guard dogs throwing themselves against a chain link fence. What they want more than anything is relief, to be set free, to tear the throat out of the thing that torments them.

And, out of this horrible set of emotions, the joy of the game is born. In the freedom of that first violent crack of pads the tension leaves you like a grounded surge of electricity. It is so completely gone that you wonder if it was ever there at all. There is no nervousness, no thought of fear, after that first hit. The butterflies (more like three-foot fruit bats) are gone. Mind and body become one conglomeration of effort. Nothing is held back during an NFL game because there is no reason to do so. It seems that life can surely go no further than the game clock.

DURING

Halftime is a cruel joke. It is like the taunt of snatching a half-eaten cheeseburger away from a starving man. Even though he will get it back in just a few minutes, the emotional plummet is certain. In those twelve short minutes at halftime the body has just enough time to cool down without getting any rest. The body's systems all screech to a halt. You stop sweating. Muscles tighten. Bruises begin to swell. Torn fingernails sting. Pain seizes joints and tendons. Headaches surge.

Now more than anything else is when technical adjustments are made. On occasion a coach may spew forth an irate speech, but they are rare.

I remember one threatening outburst.

"You sons of bitches better get your heads out of your asses! If I see an effort like what I saw in that first half again, I'll personally hit somebody in the head with the damn bench. And you bastards better believe that I'll cut some of your asses on Monday! I mean it! Now get your asses moving!"

One of my favorites was a Jerry Glanville speech when we were getting hammered by the 49ers.

"This game is over," he told us. "I know and you know we aren't going to win and I don't care. I will tell you this though. I'm not going to look at the first half of this game on film and you won't see it either. As far as I'm concerned, this thing never happened. But I'll tell you this. I'm gonna look at this second half and see who's with me. I'm gonna look to see who's still playing, even though this thing is out of reach. If you lay down on me, you're finished. If you go out there and fight your asses off, we'll be okay. We may lose this, but if you fight, there'll be another day."

We did, and there was. The next season we went on to sweep the 49ers, beating them twice, earning a playoff berth, and eliminating them from the postseason for about the only time in the last decade.

During a winning effort, a coach may sound like an indigent gold miner who's just struck the vein of a mother lode.

"We got 'um! We got 'um right where we want 'um! Now don't let go! Let's just get back out there and finish these bastards off!" (The only thing ever missing was a bellowing *Yahoooo!*)

More than any motivational speeches, it is strategy that must be addressed during halftime, plays that must be stopped, coverages that must be changed, blocks that must be made. Players are urged to drink. If necessary, quart bags of IV fluid are slugged into veins with needles that seem the size of ballpoint pens. Occasionally, some madman will slam down some stadium food, nachos, dogs, or sodas, but only if his stomach is made of cast iron. Most players are leaning back against some wall or locker, panting, dazed, with their heads lolled to one side or the other, like a bunch of convicts catching their breath after a jailbreak.

As soon as the last switch in the body is thrown down and exhaustion has fully registered in the brain, the two-minute warning comes. Everyone rises slowly, shaking and stretching the blood back into their joints and limbs. Even though a player now feels like an old jalopy with a worn-out battery, winding up its motor on a cold November morning, in just two minutes he will be running at full speed once more. When the ball is kicked high and long and the second half begins, the gears are all whining in a panicked chorus of energy. The rage and determination are right where they were when you left the field only a few minutes ago. If a guy jammed his fist under your face mask on the last play of the first half, you will be sure to forearm his ear hole on the first play of the second. Everyone picks up where he left off. There is none of the anxiety of pregame. This was nothing more than an ill-conceived pit stop.

AFTER

Depending on the outcome of the contest, the locker room is either a celebration or a morgue.

In the moments after a win, every burden is lifted from your soul. Even concerns in your life that have nothing to do with football melt and are washed away by the liquor of victory. Animosities among teammates and coaches and owners are forgotten. Everyone is everyone else's best friend. Faces are bumped on the hard plastic of shoulder pads as hugs are exchanged without concern. Sweat-drenched torsos and limbs are clasped, shaken, and entwined, players sing and dance and laugh. They hug. If it's a really big win, they might even kiss. Surly coaches let down their guard. They smile. Their eyes twinkle. It doesn't get any better than this.

The team bows their heads together. They pray. They thank God for the elation of winning and ask for the healing of the inevitable wounds. Some coaches let their team soak up the flavor of victory. They tell their men to enjoy the next twenty-four hours until next week's enemy is drawn in their sights. Some coaches think five minutes of joy is enough. Winning is expected. Only schoolgirls are giddy with celebration. There are more games left to play and things need to get much better.

The press comes in like a tidal wave spilling cameras and men and microphones everywhere. They pool in front of lockers occupied by the stars of the day. Everything is good. Everyone is happy. Congratulations are given out as freely as handbills on a city street. Even the worst errors that were made are whitewashed by the win.

After a loss the gloom hangs like a thick fog. Heads are drooped, and pain throbs unchecked by the depression of too little effort too late, or not enough at all. Some coaches chastise their men, handing out threats like bad report cards on the last day of school. "Some of you won't be here for long," they say. Nothing could be more ominous.

Some fools blame the officials. "We were robbed

outright," they'll say. Okay, but it doesn't really matter, does it?

Some coaches are hopeful, encouraged by the effort, and not wanting to push any noses too far into the stink of a loss. "Next week we get another chance," they say. "We'll get better. The effort was good. We just came up short. We'll work harder. We can do it."

But that is no consolation. The fear of reproach, of being cut or demoted, haunts every minute of a player's existence between the time the game was lost and the time the team watches the game film. Mistakes are magnified a hundred times by a loss. A missed tackle, a dropped pass, suddenly takes on epic proportions. People lose jobs over things like that. The dread can only be purged by the biting criticisms of the coaches that lance these festering wounds.

Press interviews are given in solemn mumbles. Players look to the floor when they speak. Responses come from a can. "We just didn't get the job done." "We can't give up that many points on defense and expect to win." "They played really well." "Turnovers killed us." Players are burdened with the shame of not being good enough, and only quietly hopeful that things will get better. In the showers there is no laughter. There is no singsong chatter about where to go to celebrate, only subdued whispers about the best place to quietly drown their sorrows and their woes.

When the victor leaves the locker room, he has a spring in his gait. Even if only for a day, he has elevated himself in the eyes of the world. He is a winner. For the loser, his feet feel weighted in blocks of concrete. He is somehow lower than the lowest, open for ridicule and criticism from every quarter. But this too doesn't last. There is always next week to worry about. Every veteran of the NFL knows the saying: You're only ever as good as your last game. How true.

What Players Have Forgotten About the Fans

When it comes to fans, most players would rather shake hands with a leper. In the inner circles of professional athletes, nothing is lower on the food chain than a "fan." A fan is a nonparticipator, a watcher, a wannabe, a stiff in a shirt with an outdated tie, a goofy guy wearing a matching team hat and jacket with his arm outstretched, holding on to a crummy little piece of notebook paper and a pen. Gosh, shucks, golly-gee, can I have your autograph? Players go to great lengths to avoid fans. They duck. They dodge. They wear disguises. They sneak out of back doors. They feign sight and hearing loss.

There are some things that no fan has a right to do. No fan has a right to call a player at home. Fans should also leave a player's wife and kids alone. If they love a player or hate him, they should keep it to themselves when the player's family is around. A player's family doesn't see him as a player, they just see him as their dad, husband, or son, and they can't be expected to understand. Fans do, however, have the right inside the stadium to boo and scream their fool heads off when a player screws up. But they have no right to throw things like cups of beer or disposable cameras.

In fact, if they do they should be arrested, or beaten with their own shoes.

For the most part, players just want to be left alone. They want to do their job, play the game, and collect their paychecks. They don't want people pointing and poking at them. During training camp they don't want to stop to sign their name one hundred times between the practice field and the dining hall. After a game, they don't want to have to fake a smile two dozen times to have their picture taken next to everyone's out-of-town aunt Martha. I believe, however, that these inconveniences are just part of being an NFL player. If they want their big paychecks (and they do), then players have to realize who's putting the money in the bank.

Part of earning that paycheck is signing autographs. Players should never be allowed to get paid for giving autographs. They've already been paid for that by the kid who bought the team cap, or the mom who bought the stuff she saw advertised during a game, or by the guy who forked over half a month's paycheck for season tickets. These people collectively make it possible for some players to earn as much as two hundred thousand dollars *a week*. That buys a hell of a lot of autographs, and any player cashing his check owes it to the fans to sign their cards, caps, T-shirts, or even cocktail napkins. That's part of the trade-off.

But, on the other hand, fans have to know when and where to ask for a signature. Anywhere within a mile radius of the stadium or the practice facility, players should be considered fair game. Once a player has his helmet on, or right before a game, he's off-limits. Even if he wants to sign autographs in the stadium, if it's too close to kickoff, coaches will get irate if they see a player signing programs instead of focusing on the game.

I used to be sick to my stomach when some kid leaned over the railing before a game asking me for my autograph. There were few things I wanted to do more than sign his program. Problem was, if I got caught, my position coach would chew my ear to a bloody nub. After the game, hey, it was always okay to stop and sign, and that's what I always did. I think most guys do the same.

If a player is in a restaurant, a fan can ask for an autograph at the bar, but only one, and then move on. The player is there to have drinks and dinner, not listen to a fan's opinions about football. If the player is having dinner, leave him alone. Let the poor guy eat. A friendly hello and a wave is fine, but don't ever stop at a player's table expecting to talk. Get a life.

Within the parameters I've just mentioned, fans should never have to feel embarrassed asking for an autograph. It is their right. Players who refuse should be fined five hundred dollars per incident by the league. It made me ill one time to see a little eight-year-old boy tentatively approach a football player before an awards dinner with his trading card and his marker asking for an autograph only to be rudely spurned. That kid will never forget the humiliation of that moment and his image of sports and its heroes was tarnished forever. It should have been. Asking for an autograph or a handshake, especially for a kid, can be either a lifelong memory or a nightmare. No player has the right to be the spoiler of those dreams, even if he's having a bad day himself. Fans are the ones who make the noise. Fans are the ones who pay the bills. It all starts with the kids. They are the most important fans a sport can have. Players should never forget.

NFL Physicians:
The Ultimate Conflict
of Interest

Some of the best people I met in my NFL career were team physicians. Our own orthopedic surgeon was a man of letters. He spoke six languages. He read voraciously and could talk about everything from Proust to Hemingway. He was the kind of man who loved opera and fine art museums. Yet, like so many people who are part of NFL organizations, he also had a taste for the art of violence. Because in all of art, a Francis Bacon painting, a Beethoven symphony, or even a Shakespearean murder, there is no poignancy quite as powerful as the real-life drama of men crushing one another in a real physical contest.

Despite their appreciation for the game, every NFL physician must grapple with an overwhelming conflict of interest. A doctor's loyalty is owed to whom? To his patient, of course. But an NFL physician is paid not by the patient, but by the team. The team decides if the doctor is part of the organization or not. This is no small matter either. A doctor who serves an NFL team has to worry more about how he will handle the influx of patients rather than where his next meal is coming

214

from. When lawyers, movie stars, and corporate CEOs injure themselves on the slopes of Aspen, it is an NFL doctor they want to fix them. It makes sense too. NFL doctors have ample opportunity to practice their craft, since serious injuries are as common as field goals. And NFL doctors have to get their player-patients up and running faster and better than their suburban counterparts mending the limbs of housewives and accountants. So everyone wants to see them. Working on NFL players is the best advertising a doctor could hope for.

But it is exactly the speed with which a doctor must get a player up and running that creates the potential problem. The best thing for the player is not always the best thing for the team. The team may need its middle linebacker to help stop the running game of an upcoming opponent. However, the middle linebacker may have a shoulder that could use two more weeks of rest. What happens then is fuzzy. If the doctor was advising a postman with the same injury, he might insist that he take two more weeks off work. But for a football player, well, the team needs him. If a doctor becomes too conservative with the players, he won't be around long. No team wants its players coddled. They pay big money and they expect players to swallow their fair share of pain. If this course leads to more permanent injury, again the thinking goes, that's what players get paid for.

Don't get me wrong, doctors don't coerce players into going out on the field. They don't have to. Players have been conveniently conditioned their entire lives to take the pain and put their bodies at risk. Players beg doctors for needles that numb and drugs that reduce swelling and pain. Go ahead and treat them like a race horse or a fighting pit bull. They'll do almost anything humanly possible to get out onto the field. Only the elite players can afford to be immune from this diseased way of thinking and even most of them would do the same thing.

Sometimes, though, players don't get the entire picture. I know one NFL player who had a problem with the nerves that went from his neck through his shoulder and down his arm. He was experiencing pain and weakness throughout the area. He was told to just keep going. Then he did something that, believe it or not, not a lot of players do. He asked for a second opinion. Now, NFL teams look at second medical opinions about the same way you might look at the bottom of your shoe after walking through a cow pasture. Players have a right to these second opinions under the collective bargaining agreement. Teams even have to pay for them.

When the player I'm talking about got his second opinion, he learned that one of the cartilage disks between two of the vertebrae in his neck was herniated. The unnaturally odd new shape of the disk was putting undue pressure on the nerve that serviced his shoulder and arm. Not only did the second doctor recommend that he have surgery immediately, he informed the player that the condition was visible on X-rays that the team had taken two years earlier when the player first complained of this ailment. The disk was removed and a piece of the player's hip bone was used to fuse the two remaining vertebrae together, making it safe for him to play the very next season, which he did.

Stories like that are not uncommon. Still, I do not wish to condemn NFL physicians. They are human. Like everyone else, they make mistakes, probably fewer than most. In fact, I was disturbed by a book that came out a few years ago by Dr. Robert Huizenga, the one-time L.A. Raiders team physician. Huizenga chronicled the drug use, the playing with pain, and the get-well-quick mentality of the NFL. He cited cases he'd seen firsthand where coaches, owners, and players themselves put inordinate pressure on the players' bodies to perform despite what may have been in the best interest of their health. My problem with Huizenga is this: How is it that he served as a physician in this difficult situation at all? If he was so appalled, why didn't he leave? Why did he wait until he was safely ensconced in a Beverly Hills medical practice before he cried foul?

I know why physicians can serve as NFL team doctors and still sleep at night. The conflict is there, but there is certainly an easy rationalization to alleviate any feelings of guilt. Players, coaches, and management push the players to get back on the field, not the doctors. If players are willing to compromise their long-term well-being for the big financial rewards of the NFL, then, the thinking goes, it's their choice. However, any team doctor must know that he is walking a thin line between loyalties. Certainly a doctor has the obligation to fully inform a player of the severity of every injury, and of any long-term debilities that might result from getting back onto the field too soon. If he fails in this, he has failed to adhere to his duties as a physician and a decent human being. After he's apprised a player fully and honestly of the situation, he bears no further responsibilty. The players can then choose for themselves.

WHY PLAYERS
HAVE LUCKY SOCKS

Winning in the NFL is so tenuous that players will travel to the distant boundaries of reason in hopes of giving themselves and their team that little edge they need to put them over the top. Despite the numerous plays (about one hundred and fifty) executed during a typical game, winning and losing usually comes down to one, two, or three simple errors and strokes of luck. Seven, or snake eyes. It is the nightmare of every player, every week, to have that tiny sprinkling of bad luck fall on him at such a critical moment and have to shoulder that excruciating burden of loss through the upcoming days. A string of such bad luck can mean the end of a career. One guy I know missed a single block on a kickoff return. Even the best special teams player will miss this kind of block five out of ten times. The bad luck was that the defender he missed went on down the field to smash into Tim Brown, the Raiders' star receiver, and take out his knee. It was just bad luck that this guy's small error resulted in an injury to a star player. That little bit of bad luck cost him his career. And so, superstition has a fertile breeding ground in the NFL.

With many players securing luck is as simple as wearing the same pair of socks, a chain, an earring, jock, T-shirt, or gloves week in and week out. It's when these articles can't be cleaned for fear of washing the luck right out of them that things become odorous. But these distractions are nothing more than simple substitutes for rabbits' feet. It is when players begin to think that they must reenact the exact sequence of events from the previous week when victory was attained that things become difficult. These sequences may be something as simple as the order in which a player dresses himself before a game, or as complex as who sits where on the airplane and what is served for dinner on Saturday night. Deion Sanders insists on laying out his entire uniform on the floor, as if someone were lying there wearing it, but had suddenly disappeared into thin air. Then he meticulously dresses himself from his socks to his helmet in the exact same order week after week.

I'd like to say my own sense of logic superseded any superstitions, but I can't. One thing I would never do was look into a mirror once I was dressed in my uniform for a game. This crazy notion dated back to when I was an athlete in high school. I believed that a football player, or a wrestler, should never be worried about what he looked like. One day before a wrestling match, I shrugged this notion off and looked admiringly at myself in the mirror for several minutes, flexing my arms and straightening out the creases in my uniform. I got my tail handed to me in the ensuing match and would never look in the mirror again right up until my last days in the NFL.

Most players won't knowingly ignore their own important good luck rituals. Terry Bradshaw did once and it almost cost him Super Bowl XIV.

"The two things I always had to do were sing the national anthem and go to the chapel service before the game," Bradshaw told me.

I can't tell you why Terry missed the chapel service the day before one of the most important games of his life, he swore me to secrecy, so you'll have to ask him yourself. Needless to say, it had something to do with the previous night's activities. Terry threw three interceptions that day.

"I knew God was gonna hammer me," he recalled.

The strangest ritual I ever heard of was Mark van Eeghen's. Van Eeghen was the Oakland Raiders' star fullback in the 1970s and 1980s. It seems one day before a game he and roommate Dave Casper were fooling around, wrestling in their hotel room. During one sequence of professional-like moves and throws, van Eeghen climbed up on top of the TV and launched himself onto the bed. The next day he had a hundred-yard game. Thereafter, van Eeghen was reported to not have felt comfortable going into a game unless he had launched himself off the TV onto his hotel bed before the contest.

Matt Millen, also an All-Pro Raiders player, made the mistake of cracking Art Shell's back before a game one time. The Hall of Fame offensive lineman and team captain played so well he would appear every game thereafter in front of Matt's locker.

"He wouldn't say a thing," Matt said. "He'd just look at me and nod his head, then fall backward. I would have to catch him and crack his back. Art would never get on a scale, but I know he was about three-thirty. I'd see spots after catching him and then having to lift him off his feet to crack his back. I was glad when he finally retired. I don't know how long I could have kept going like that."

Superstition isn't just relegated to the individual players. If a team wins, superstition dictates that everything has to be the same the next week in order to preserve the edge. In Atlanta, we had a coach who would sing or not sing "Mack the Knife" in the team meeting on Saturday nights in the hotel depending on the outcome of the previous week's game and whether or not he sang.

Players insist on riding with the same people to the airport or the stadium. They dress the same way. They'll listen to the same music. They'll eat the same exact food in the same exact order, eggs, then pancakes, then spaghetti, and maybe make sure they get some of the syrup on the noodles. They'll read the same stories to their kids at night during the week, or date the same girls they did the week before. Any variation on a winning week's sequence of events is known to be an egg in the face of lady luck and an invitation to disaster. Coaches buy into it just as much as players. This can be a tremendous advantage. If, for instance, a coach had an easy week of practice during a victorious week, players will lobby for, and oftentimes win, the same reprieve from harsh contact and after-practice sprints for the next week as well.

Granted, some teams seem to be beyond luck or beyond the help of luck. But most NFL seasons are filled with teams in the middle of the pack. A loss or two can mean the firing of an entire coaching staff and the reshuffling of players. An extra win may result in a playoff bid and big contract extensions for everyone. In one way, it's laughable that careers and seasons could hinge on a dirty jock strap. But if players and coaches believe that their peculiar adherence to lucky charms really will help, then maybe it is that mental predisposition to thinking they'll be lucky that really does tilt the balance between success and failure. Right or wrong, I don't think there is now or ever was a single player in the NFL, no matter how rational a thinker, who doesn't succumb to the tempting narcotic of superstition.

What NFL Players on Opposite Sides of the Line Say to Each Other During a Game

I don't want you to get the wrong idea. During the four or five seconds of a play, from when the ball is snapped until the whistle is blown, there are no friends among opposing players in the game of football. During a play, if one friend could knock his buddy on the other team unconscious, he'd be happy. People who don't understand that, don't get to play in the NFL. Taking it easy on someone, or holding back for any reason, is for the backyard games. In the NFL, it's destroy or be destroyed. Because every player knows this, there are no hard feelings.

The exception of course is for the guys who play dirty. Yet, even then, if protocol is followed, and apologies are issued, guys will begrudgingly accept dirty tricks. The protocol is that if you're coached to play dirty, then you tell your opposing buddy beforehand that you're sorry, but it's either whip his legs, or you lose your job. He'll understand. He has to. Every NFL player knows what it means to get directives from a coach. For the majority of players, you either do it, or you may not be around. For good clean hits that leave people unconscious or reeling in pain, well, it's like fighting brothers, whether it's black eyes or broken bones, when the fight's over, everybody loves each other.

Knowing that, it won't surprise you that the dialogue that goes on between players during a game can be quite pleasant, depending entirely on the relationship between the two men. With free agency flipping players between teams like trading cards between neighborhood kids, it's very common for opposing players to be friends. Two guys who lived together on the road for four years who may not have seen each other for a year can suddenly find themselves faced off across the line of scrimmage. If they do, a dialogue not unlike the kind you'd expect to hear during a backyard barbecue might unfold over the course of a game. Talk about wives and kids might give way to commonly held investments and then evolve into a discussion on the merits of working for their respective organizations: How hard was training camp? Is the quarterback really a drunk? Does the coach throw things in meetings?

One game we Falcons played Green Bay, and I had the chance to hit Brett Favre, the Packers' quarterback, just as he got off a pass. Even though I was lying there on top of him after just smashing him to the turf, Brett said to me quite pleasantly, "Hey Tim, how are you?"

Bret and I were roommates for a while on the road when he was a rookie in Atlanta, and we always liked each other.

"Good, Brett," I replied. "How about you?"

"Good."

"Look," I said, aware that while we were conversing one of my teammates had intercepted his ball and was running around the field like a mouse in a snake pit, "I've got to block you, you know. That's why I'm not letting you up."

"That's okay," he said, trying to struggle against me only briefly before realizing he was hopelessly pinned.

Then the play was over.

"I'll see you later," I said, getting up and jogging away.

"I hope not until after the game," he told me.

Because players switch from team to team, there is a feeling of camaraderie in the NFL that doesn't exist in college where almost everyone is locked into one team for four or five years and everyone else is the enemy. Besides players who are traded back and forth, many guys from across the NFL get to know one another during the off-season at events like the Pro Bowl, NFLPA-sponsored vacations, and charity fund-raisers. Also in the NFL, there is a common enemy for players: management. It isn't a blood feud, but anytime you get two groups of men on opposite sides of a stack of money, they aren't going to gravitate toward each other naturally. Because NFL players see themselves as having to fight together to get their fair share of the revenue pie, they inherently unite.

With this tacit fraternity in place, candid conversations erupt between players even if they haven't before met. Players on both sides of the line study each other during film meetings all week. They know how opposing players move and how they play the game. Even for two guys who have never played against each other before, they feel like they know each other, as if they've met in a dream. Depending on the guys, like everything else, some people are shy, some are gregarious, two opposing players may go the entire game in silence, or they may greet each other with grunts of hello on the first play. When the game gets out of reach, everybody loosens up. That's when the friendliest talking occurs. Guys on both sides know when it's over, and when that happens, the biggest concern everyone has is not getting injured.

My most vivid conversation in the NFL was with Kent Hull and Jim Ritcher, two enormous and ill-tempered linemen with the Buffalo Bills. I don't know how they had my number, but they had it. They not only had the advantage as offensive players of knowing the snap count, they seemed to also know the direction I was going before I knew myself. And there were two of them against me. And they were bigger. And they were stronger. It was ugly. They whipped me, and pummeled me, and ground me into the turf. After each running play, I would get a little lower in my stance and jump a little faster at the snap of the ball, abandoning all pretense of doing anything but getting around and thus away from these two human sausage grinders. Finally, I backed right off the ball so far the linebacker was kicking my heels. The ball was snapped, it was a sweep to the left. I raced that way. I had them beat. I heard them curse and then I felt two hooks snatch the back of my jersey and yank so hard that the back of my head was the first thing to hit the ground.

I got up slowly. The play was already over.

"Isn't it bad enough," I said, looking up at them through the iron bars of their masks, "that you guys have pummeled me all game and you're beating us by five touchdowns? Now I finally get away and you grab me from behind like this is the World Wrestling Federation."

The two of them snickered like preteen girls at a slumber party.

"You're too quick," one of them grumbled.

"Yeah," said the other, "if you weren't so quick, we wouldn't have to grab you. But we're not lettin' you go. We'd catch hell . . ."

In the movies, players scream and grunt at each other

like maniacs. When guys do that kind of Hollywood stuff in real life, everyone else rolls their eyes. Players on that guy's own team are embarrassed and let the opposing players know that they too think their vociferous teammate is an ass. For the most part, players are too busy concentrating on their exact responsibilities to do too much jawing, but when they do talk, it isn't about each other's momma. That kind of crap could get you killed.

The worst exchange of words I ever had was with the 49ers' All-Pro offensive guard, Guy McIntyre. McIntyre was always a mean player, even though he is a very religious guy off the field. He'd always give you that extra shove at the end of a play, and he seemed to take special delight in performing the repertoire of dirty 49er tricks. One play, he and I got into a shoving match after the whistle.

"Fuck you!" he said.

"No, fuck you," I told him.

"Fuck you!"

"Fuck you too!"

I don't know how long this would have gone on if a ref hadn't stepped between us and started making threats. Of course, seeing it on the written page I realize how ridiculous the whole thing was.

My point though is that after the game, McIntyre was waiting for me outside the tunnel.

"Sorry," he said, shaking my hand. "You know how it is."

"Yeah," I told him. "No big deal."

And it wasn't. It almost never is.

IT'S ONLY BUSINESS

One thing NFL players don't understand is the mind-set of the NFL corporate executives. To the players, the people of the league are the bad guys, nothing but suits occupying Park Avenue suites paid for by the players' sweat and blood. To the NFL players, the league executives are nothing but minions of the greedy owners. It's not true.

NFL executives share a common bond with players that the players don't even realize: their love of football. The executives of the NFL think that they have the best jobs in the world. They're constantly around the game of football. They're sports fans. They high-five each other and pat each other on the back like Super Bowl champions over the knowledge that they have watched NFL football become the number one sport in America. But they're not satisfied with just that. They want to make NFL football the number one sport in the entire world. They'll do it too.

The league has well-thought-out plans of overseas expansion. One day you will see NFL teams in Europe and South America. Asia will follow when someone solves the problems of travel and time zones. I'm not talking about the World League either. The World League is simply a precursor to real NFL teams abroad.

But right now the league executives are simply looking overseas. They're very cognizant of the problems the NFL is potentially facing here at home. One concern is a shrinking talent pool. Title IX (the NCAA mandate that requires equal funding for women's sports) will continue to erode football programs except at only the biggest of colleges, and football teams are becoming harder and harder to field in both high schools and Little Leagues for budgetary reasons as well as misperceptions among American mothers. Most people think soccer is a safer alternative for kids even though every orthopedic surgeon I've spoken with tells me there are more injuries to children playing soccer than there are in football. The NFL leadership has their heads out of the sand on this issue and are already considering how to arrest these trends. They know they will need more and more highly skilled players in order to have successful expansion abroad. As far as expansion within this country, don't look for that to happen again until at least 2005. The people that run the league are smart. They've got a good thing going and they don't want to saturate their market with too many teams.

I know players are going to think I've turned on them for even having two good words to say about the people who run the league. Players and management are like lions and jackals. The players' distaste is inherently blind. More than anything, the animosity is bred from the players' knowledge that their careers will be short-lived and that even without them the league and its stewards will go on, making money, and reaping the rewards. Players have to get over this. The NFL has tried to build bridges to players with its continuing-education program, job internship program, and teacher-of-the-year program that honors teachers who had a special impact on their lives. Some players think these programs are nothing more than public relations efforts by a big business. Well, even if they're right, the programs are real and they do serve players. The other thing players have to get over is that the people who run the NFL are simply businessmen, and they're good at what they do. I know sometimes it hurts, if you're one of the players whose body is battered, whose bank account is empty, and whose career has ended too soon, but you have to remember, it's only business.

The Best and Worst Places to Play in the NFL

When players talk about NFL stadiums they're not concerned with cushioned seats or plenty of peanuts for the fans. Players are preoccupied with the atmosphere. This means the type of crowd, the condition of the field, the feel of the tunnels, the locker room, and the landscape.

BUFFALO

The strangest place to go as a player is Buffalo. It's like landing on a different planet and being welcomed (or unwelcomed) by an alien nation. Your bus takes you from downtown Buffalo along the edge of Lake Erie and out to the suburbs where the stadium is. During that ride, you pass enormous old mills, warehouses, and factories. Most of these are nothing more than hulking abandoned shells, like the burnt-out destroyed spacecraft of an earlier invasion by a gigantic race that failed just as you too will surely fail. It's hard to win in Buffalo.

Every time I've been there, the very sky has been otherworldly, dark, ominous, billowing piles of gray smoke stacked for miles above you, obliterating even a hint of sun, another harbinger of the defeat to come. When your bus nears the stadium, you notice that the roadways are lined with strange humanoid forms, bare to their waists, with red- and blue-colored skin carelessly exposed to the unkind elements. They shriek at you to go home. They spit. They throw cups of beer. They make wildly obscene signs with their hands, mouths, and feet. As the stadium comes into view, so does a regiment of Buffalo's finest: aerodynamic homes that move, spacecraft sprouting antennae and flying brazen flags of red and blue in the cold wind. Outside these craft, open pits burn out of control, searing meat of unknown origin as it slowly turns on metal spits. More aliens shriek. They wail. Go home. You'd like nothing more. But now it's too late and they feed you to their team. The Bills grind you up like a crude sausage machine. The crowd jeers. It begins to rain. You look at the clock and think about a warm bath at home, eight hundred miles away, on a different planet.

PHILADELPHIA

Philadelphia is known by almost every player in the league as the most hostile place to play. The crowds there make the Buffalo people seem like troops of Boy Scouts. Their mouths are so foul and so loquacious that they could make whores blush. The field too is the most inhospitable in the league. Seams crisscross the artificial surface like poorly disguised jungle booby traps.

CHICAGO

Soldier Field is the stuff dreams are made of. The neo-classical columns and friezes that rise up from behind the excited crowds transport you to the days of Rome when gladiator slaves battled to win the right to be free men. The turf is in fact turf. It smells like a freshly cut back lawn on a summer morning. The wind is always a factor. The team plays hard and mean, but they're the type of guys who would take you out for a beer after the contest, if such a tradition was cultivated by the NFL. Across the street is the Field Museum. On the other side is the water's edge, Lake Michigan, the Shedd Aquarium, and the city's planetarium. This stadium is a true civic center and if they ever move the Bears' playing site to the suburbs or inside a dome, Mike McCaskey should be run out of town on a rail.

SAN FRANCISCO

The disturbing thing about San Francisco is the type of fan they attract. The tickets for these events are among the costliest in the league. People who own season passes to these coveted events are as likely to have two or three degrees hanging on the den wall at home as one. It is an educated and well-to-do crowd. This is disturbing because of the way they behave, like maniacs. Crude and rude. You can be sure to hear taunting from the people in the front row on the fifty-yard line. Their comments may not be as vile as the ones you hear in Philadelphia, but what the San Francisco crowd lacks in depravity, they make up for with relentlessness. There's something truly unsettling about having a high-tech executive dressed in a button-down Ralph Lauren shirt with a matching sweater slung around his shoulders screaming with red-faced ire, *"Green, you suck!"*

Rest at ease though, once outside the stadium walls these same fans revert to mild-mannered Americans. I once ventured out into the parking lot after a game to purchase a six-pack of beer for the bus ride to the airport from some tailgaters and I was treated like the prodigal son. They refused my money, and sent me back to the bus laden not only with cold beer, but sandwiches and polite wishes of good luck for the rest of the season.

THE MEADOWLANDS

Football in a can. This is no stadium, it's a facility. It's set in the middle of the swamps outside Newark, New Jersey, that is. The neighborhood is a Superfund nightmare. The grass is plastic. The rain is dirty. During Giants games, some fans wear Jets colors. During Jets games some fans wear Giants colors. Curse the Giants for ever leaving Yankee Stadium. This place reminds me of a disposable razor. I can't wait until they throw it away. Go home to New York, both of you.

CLEVELAND

Here's a place you don't mind getting shouted at. It's what you expect from the fans in Cleveland. Drive through the city and outside the wonderfully Gothic downtown square and you'll see factories that belch real fire from their stacks. The stadium itself is run-down. The water pressure in the showers is worse than at a mountain campsite. The locker room is crowded. The steel of the structure is rusted. The concrete is damp. The field, although meritoriously grass, comes up in clumps the size of a large pizza. Dog biscuits rain down on your helmet from the end zone area known as "The Dog Pound." That's okay. You wouldn't expect anything less. Again, wind and clouds and sometimes rain or even snow are part of the experience. This is football for real people.

ANAHEIM

God bless St. Louis. I can even forgive their dome. Anaheim was no place to play football. It was a baseball stadium. The sun always shined. The crowds were anemic. Smog hung in the air like the must of an attic. Once the plumbing backed up during the game and afterward there was six inches of raw sewage on the locker room floor. I don't have to say it.

GREEN BAY

This is the kind of place where people stand quietly before the national anthem, and then sing. There is no wild cheering until the last words of the song have ceased to echo. This is the kind of place that claps politely when an opposing player is carried off the field. Instead of hot dogs, people eat brats with mustard. Going to Green Bay is like stepping forty years back in time. It's a pleasure.

MILE HIGH

Here too the people are like the neighbors in a small town during the holidays. They wear the colors of the team, a sea of orange and blue. The elevation is so high that it feels like someone sucked the air from your lungs with an industrial vacuum. Just running out onto the field from the sideline makes you delirious, so it's hard to appreciate the lovely snowcapped mountain range in the distance beyond the stadium walls.

RFK

This stadium is set on the wrong side of the tracks in D.C. with the highway on one side and the tenements on the other. That whole end of town is getting run-down and the stadium isn't immune from the blight. The concrete tunnels ooze dank slime. That's okay. The field is grass. Even the tightest coach in the league will let his players have a few hours the day before the game to see the memorials. Most teams stay at the L'Enfante Plaza, and the ride to the stadium from there takes you through the European architecture of our country's capital in all its grandeur, past the Smithsonian, the Capitol, and the Supreme Court. You can feel the power.

DOMES

If you've been to one, you've been to them all.

FAXES, PHONES, AND PHOTOS . . . ON THE SIDELINE

At least once, during almost every NFL game, I'd be sitting there on the bench, heaving to catch my breath, and I'd hear ringing in my ears. This wasn't always the result of having tried to tackle some freight train like Ironhead Heyward or Jerome Bettis. More often than that, it was the telephone. Someone would get up slowly and go to the table where the Gatorade was standing in cups waiting to be consumed and pick up the ringing phone.

"Tim," they'd say, "it's for you."

Slowly I'd get up. The news on the phone during a game is rarely good. Most times, it was my defensive line coach, Bill Kolar, barking obscenities at me and everyone, urging us to get underneath a certain trap block, make a certain tackle, stay home on the bootleg, or get to the quarterback faster. Half the coaching staff is up in the press box during a game, surveying the action from up high and scouting the enemy for weaknesses and tendencies. Their only connection to us is Ma Bell.

But the phone isn't always used to chastise players. Sometimes, if you make a play that's so good your coach just can't contain himself, he'll call down to tell you he loves you. They do that, coaches. They're like high school girlfriends. They can hate you one minute, and love you the next. And, like the sappy adolescent boyfriend, you always answer the phone. Although, I admit that I saw a guy once refuse to get on the phone. Kolar wanted to talk to Mike Gann, a fellow defensive lineman, I mean scream at him, and Gann knew it. Gann had blown the last play on the field and it ended up with the other team scoring a touchdown. He refused to answer.

"Tell him I'm not talking to him," Gann replied calmly.

Touché. It was the thing I always wanted to do, as an adolescent, and as an NFL player. But I never had the nerve.

Phones are used for strategic adjustments as well. Quarterbacks will get on the line with the offensive coordinator to talk about the weaknesses in the defense's coverage, the adjustments they are making, and how best to capitalize during the next series. Coaches will oftentimes request information from players to get a better insight as to what's happening, what stunts or plays the players think might work, or to monitor the mood of their squad.

But when you talk about strategy, no two pieces of high-tech equipment are more beneficial than the quarterback radio and the thermo-fax. The quarterback radio allows one coach from each team to talk directly into the helmet of the quarterback. Usually the offensive coordinator or the head coach, this coach can even change the plays at the line of scrimmage if he sees something the quarterback himself is missing. The only limitation is that when the play clock reaches fifteen seconds, the transmission is automatically cut off. (The play clock counts down either forty-five seconds from the end of the previous play or twenty-five seconds from the time when the ball was reset on the field if it was run out of bounds or an incomplete pass was thrown.) The radio goes only one way, so the quarterback cannot talk back to the coaches. Also, the coach talking to the quarterback must be on the sideline, and not up high in the stadium's coaching booth. It should be noted, however, that the coach up in the box can relay some bit of information to the coach on the sideline through the headsets that connect all coaches. The sideline coach can then call the adjustment seen by the guy up in the box into the quarterback's helmet. This isn't typical because the means of communication is so convoluted, but it does happen from time to time.

The thermo-fax is commonly known as a video printer. It is not allowed inside the bench area, but you can usually see it set up just outside that area, on the field, between the bench and the stands. The league has banned this high-tech equipment from the immediate area of the players to avoid the image of an electronic control center, but its influence is still the same. The thermo-fax takes pictures directly from the team's coaching cameras on the fifty-yard line and in the end zone. The end zone camera usually delivers three still shots of the field, one wide shot before the play to show the formation, one zoom in on the linemen to show their stances, and another shot about three seconds after the ball has been snapped to show the development of the play. The sideline camera usually delivers two still shots, both wide, one before the play and another three seconds after the ball is snapped.

These fax-photos are used to do a quick analysis of the play that just took place, and five of them are electronically zipped down to the field after every play. Coaches use these pictures to show players what happened, or what didn't happen. Lots of times, things happen so fast and the action is so disorienting on the field that players don't know if they were hit by the guard or the fullback, or even if the ball was carried inside of them or outside of them. The fax can be a player's best friend or his worst enemy. It can confirm that he was where he should have been, or convict him of failing to do his job. It's not that big a deal though. A player who does something wrong knows he'll get caught sooner or later anyway. Even if the fax doesn't provide the evidence of his culpability, Monday morning, the coach's film in its entirety will.

The balance the league is trying to strike with these high-tech gadgets is between optimum performance on the field on one side, and avoiding the evolution of an oversized board game on the other. If technology is too essential, the game could boil down to a couple of old coaches sitting in their cushioned chairs in air-conditioned boxes high above the fray, directing all the action before them. Without some of these gadgets, the game is sloppier and less exciting. Right now, things are right about where they should be, a mixture of the individual efforts of players on the field and the strategic planning of coaches on the sideline and in the box. The challenge for the NFL will be to curb the exponentially advancing possibilities of instant images, complex communication, and computer analysis to keep the game of football with at least one foot in the dirt.

Then again, maybe the league has nothing to worry about. Tom Atchison, the video coordinator for the Atlanta Falcons, was the guy who first developed the use of the thermo-fax. As Falcon players, we were constantly reviewing these faxes on the sideline and consulting with our coaches via telephone. Still, they seemed to be of little use whenever it came to stopping the 49ers or the Cowboys or the Bills from drubbing us on the field. The only electrical connection it seemed we couldn't make was the one that lit up the scoreboard. In a way this is comforting, and maybe just an-other reason why people love the game of football. In our society of lawyers and letters, modems and com-puters, phones and fiber optics, it's kind of nostalgic to know there's still a place where a forearm means more than a fax.

Thoughts from a
Losing Battle

Every football player goes through it. Even the best of teams are blown out at one time or another. Granted, as an Atlanta Falcon, I experienced more than my fair share of blowouts. They were never pretty. In a way, losing a game, or a lot of games, is like having someone die. It's not as bad as that, of course, but the sickening feeling is pretty much the same. It's that moment of darkness, like a train passing through a long tunnel, when you're not completely certain you'll ever come out on the other side. With losing though, unlike when someone dies, people don't feel bad for you. In fact, people are mad at you. They insult you. You even start to wonder yourself if you're just not good enough, and that's why you're losing.

A blowout is a special kind of losing. You get to think about it much longer than a game you lose in the last few seconds. You get to absorb the feeling, soak it up like a heavy old towel. I've been in games where the outcome was determined as early as the second quarter. I know, it's never over until it's over, or not until the fat lady sings. But if you think there are games when she

241

isn't bellowing like a stuck cow before the halftime gun, then you're living in a world of fantasy. The feeling of imminent defeat can't be quantified, but it can be unmistakably identified. You know when it happens, because the light in the eyes of everyone around you is nothing more than the feeble glow from the coals of a doused campfire, where only moments before that light was a raging bonfire. It happens like that, quickly. Some guys' fires of hope burn longer than others'. That's the way it is everywhere in life. But even when the maddest optimist sees the capitulation on the faces of everyone around him, he too gives up and hangs on for the ride.

It's shameful to say it, really, that there was ever a game where I gave up hope. It seems un-American. It seems sacrilegious. It seems cowardly. But I can't lie; there were such games, where try as I might, common sense would just come blasting through that barricaded door in my mind and make me face the music, the fat lady's music. When this happens, players' thoughts go the way of those of most other men who find themselves on sinking ships: to self-preservation. For football players, it's a matter of trying not to get hurt more than anything. Injury is the plague of any player's career, more deadly than age, or an ill-tempered coach, a losing season, a fumbled punt, or a contract holdout. Injury is death in the NFL. Since injury is possible on any and every play, danger always lurks. When the game is out of reach, getting hurt is like being shipped home out of a battle zone and dying in a car accident just as you're going to pull into your driveway.

But not getting hurt is harder than it may sound. You might think it would be as simple as motoring down and watching your back. It's not. Part of not getting hurt entails going full speed. If you let up, or stop your feet from moving, you're in the most vulnerable position you can be on the football field. If your feet are planted like an oak tree and you get hit, something has to snap, usually your bones or ligaments. So you keep your feet chopping. You keep moving around the field just like you did when you cared. It's just that your primary focus is no longer so much what you hit, but how you hit it. You want to make the tackle, but not at the expense of your neck. You want to catch the ball, but not at the expense of your ribs. With everybody on the losing team thinking like this, it gets pretty ugly. The other team senses it though, and, unless there is some bitter feud between the two sides or the desire for retribution for when the shoe was on the other foot, the winning team calms down as well. They've been there. They don't want anybody to get hurt either. They've got their win and most times that's what they care about more than anything. The game becomes a series of Hollywood stunts where everyone is doing his best to make it look good, but the main objective is keeping everybody healthy. When the point spread is still within reach, these are the minutes in the game that give the gamblers their ulcers. It seems like the losing team isn't trying. It seems like the winning team isn't going for the kill. Because they aren't. Why do you think a point spread of anything more than fourteen is so rare in NFL games? It certainly isn't because a team like the 49ers doesn't have the ability to beat the Bengals by fifty points. They do.

The worst nightmare for a player is getting hurt in a blowout, in the last game of the season, where the contest is meaningless and everybody just wants to get home. We played a game like that in Atlanta one year against Detroit. Both teams had miserable seasons. We had only won three games. The temperature had dropped below zero, almost unheard of in Atlanta, and the field was frozen solid. Outside the stadium U-haul vans and trucks stuffed with boxes, bags, and suitcases filled the players' parking lot, already packed and ready to blow town the minute the game ended. When you have a miserable season, you can't get out of town fast enough. Almost every player from both sides wanted only one thing, to make it through the game unharmed. Getting hurt is bad enough when you've got to suffer through the season. But getting hurt right before the off-season begins means if you had plans to go anywhere to forget about the miserable season and recharge your batteries, you can skip it. You'll be in surgery and then rehab for the next several months.

I remember being taken out of that game in the fourth quarter. I breathed a sigh of relief as my backup went in to get some reps. I had made it through the game and through the season. Nothing was between me and the off-season when I could heal my body, then train for the next season, which would certainly be better than this one had been. It was a good feeling.

I wish I could say the same was true for all my teammates. One guy, a linebacker named John Rade, didn't get to come out late in the game. He stayed in, and, in a pileup, twisted his knee. That didn't deter him from getting home. He drove straight from that game to his home in Idaho. It took a day and a half, but he made the escape. Unfortunately, by the time Rade got home with his fully laden truck, his knee was swollen to twice its normal size. He got on a plane and headed back for Atlanta. They operated right away. He needed a total knee reconstruction and would spend the next six months in Atlanta rehabilitating his broken joint. Which just goes to show you that, try as you might, sometimes you just can't avoid getting hurt, even in a blowout, even when nobody wants to hurt anybody, even when that's the only thing you're thinking about, and believe me, it is.

This is a painful thing to think about, players giving up and thinking only of themselves. But really, if you think about it honestly, you can see the logic. Players know that when they are injured, they essentially disappear from the minds of their coaches, teammates, and fans. If you're hurt too bad, or gone too long, you never come back. The money and the fame end. You shuffle off into the next phase of life, which, chances are, you're not ready for. Players don't give a hoot about fans and gamblers who are expecting them to lay it all on the line, every minute of every game, win, lose, or draw. Same thing goes for the coaches. Every player knows that a coach is only his friend as long as he can turn in quality performances on the field. In fact, if a team has had a lousy season, and they perceive the coach as a jerk, or a loser, they secretly delight in losing those last few contests in a pitiful season. They hope that the losses will put the final nails in the coach's coffin, and that next year they'll have a new man to lead their team in a new direction. This is all the game within the game. It's the mentality that has won and lost battles during the last five thousand years of history. Now that you know the psychological intangibles of every contest, you know why winning and losing is so hard to predict. They make factoring in a point spread impossible. Makes you feel real confident about this weekend's parlay, doesn't it?

THE RIFT IN EVERY TEAM

Teamwork, it's a wonderful concept. Teamwork is something football players either learn early on, or, as when they fail to learn any of the other primary skills of the game, they aren't around long. When most people think of teamwork, however, they think of the entire team, the roster from A to Z. That's not the way it is on an NFL football team. Team unity and teamwork sound good for the fans and the media and even the coaches, but the reality is that every NFL team is divided into two distinct groups: offense and defense.

Like an uncomfortable truce between neighboring countries momentarily aligned to take on some larger foe, offensive and defensive players on an NFL team will purport to the rest of the world that they are allies, bound in a common cause. But, the truth be known, these two groups each look with disdain upon the other and consider them to be a somewhat unwanted, but tolerated set of cousins. Offensive guys think of defensive players as unpolished country cousins, crude and brash, lacking the fine skills and discipline it takes to be the part of some magnificent choreographed set of motions that make up a play that results in a touchdown, the thing every team needs to win games, and, most would argue, to fill seats in the stadium.

Defensive players, on the other hand, if pressed, would admit that offensive players are simply defensive players who possess the physical skills to play the game, but who lack the requisite toughness and meanness to be on the defensive side of the ball. Defensive players too would contend that while they are the country cousins, the offensive players are more of the city types, spoiled with rich skill, but lacking the fortitude to get down in the dirt and muddy their hands with quite the same fervor as a defensive player. And, like offensive players, defensive guys might concede it is the offensive circus acts that fill the seats, but to a man they will also tell you that it is the defense that wins the games. Certainly, the reasoning goes, if the other team can't score, they can't win.

More than any innate differences between the two groups, it is training camp and practice that breeds the most mutual contempt. For five weeks in August, and then three or four days every week during the season, these two groups, despite the fact that they are all on the same team, square off and battle each other with a fury that can only be exceeded, if at all, in an actual game. During training camp, players from both sides are expected to win their individual battles. Careers and livelihoods are on the line. There is no love lost. Eruptions of fisticuffs between offensive and defensive players during camp, where there is no risk of fifteen-yard penalties, ejections, or heavy fines, are as common as water breaks. I've seen players remove their helmets and swing them like Viking battle-axes at the heads of people they call teammates. I've heard men threaten to shoot each other and curse their mothers in a way you'd never hear during a game. These two sides build up a hatred of each other that may be camouflaged during a successful season, but it is never completely eradicated.

It is during an unsuccessful football campaign that the public is most likely to hear the rumblings of tension that exist between the two factions of a team. When the offense is performing well and scoring points, yet the team is losing because of a porous defense, you will hear offensive players hint at the inadequacy of their counterparts. When a defense, on the other hand, does a tremendous job of holding off a powerful opposing offense, only to have their own offense go out and turn the ball right back over to them again via a turnover or three unsuccessful plays, their disgust is openly vented. The best example of this was with the Cardinals during Buddy Ryan's inaugural season as head coach. Defensive players were openly berating their offensive teammates in the papers. Offensive guys publicly countered that they were the victims of a coach who played favorites and bred ill will without regard to team unity.

It is only when a team is so dominant, and so successful, that the rift goes completely unnoticed by the outside world. Even so, it exists. Defensive and offensive players typically spend their free time among themselves, in the locker room and away from team functions. Many team leaders will arrange nights out on the town for both sides to try and overcome this rift, but in most cases, even during those outings, players from the same side of the ball naturally gravitate toward each other. During a typical day, in training camp, or during the season, the two groups spend almost no time together as a cohesive unit. Team meetings, where everyone is together, are brief. After that, the day is divided down the line between the squads. It isn't crossed without an element of violence. The limited interaction between the two is on the practice field where taunting, fighting, and generally bashing each other's heads in is the rule. Even during a game, if you look carefully you will see that offensive players sit on one bench and the defensive guys sit on another, with the water table and telephones on the fifty-yard line separating the two.

Because of this rift, there are no real limits to how far the two opposing factions will go to foil each other on the practice field. In Atlanta, we would have one-on-one run-blocking drills almost every day of practice. These drills were the worst things in practice. Basically they'd line up two opposing linemen and let them smash into each other at full speed. The offensive guy would be given a directive by a coach who stood behind the defensive guy where only the offensive guy could see it. The signals would tell the offensive player whether or not he was to block the defensive guy to the left, the right, or just come straight at him with a drive block. This is a nerve-wracking experience for a defensive lineman, sitting there, with all eyes on you, and the job of reacting quick as a hiccup to what the truck in front of you is trying to do before you attempt to keep him from blowing you backward.

The scheme I invented was perfect. It was a simple code where the type of words used to encourage the man who was up in the drill would tell him the directives the offensive guy was receiving from the coach. For instance, if it was a straight-on drive block, I would yell to my fellow defensive lineman, "Come on Mike. Come on!" It sounded harmless enough, but it gave us defensive guys an incalculable advantage. Despite what everyone knew was a drill to the offense's advantage, we rarely lost these minor battles for the line of scrimmage. They hated us for beating them.

Our downfall was when one of us defensive linemen

was converted to offense. We were sunk. The traitor soon alerted the entire enemy camp to our tricks. They gloated with their newfound knowledge. Some days they would go the opposite direction of what the coach told them to do. Some days they would follow his directive exactly. We were foiled, and we hated them for gaining back the advantage we had so cunningly stolen. It didn't matter that we were thieves. It was us against them. No love lost. No holds barred. It always was. It always will be.

NFL SPIES AND TRAITORS

Although much is made of the analogy between football and war, little is made of the seamier side of either armed conflict. The truth is, football games, like battles and even wars, can be won or lost with effective spies or well-placed traitors. A spy in the NFL has never been traced back to an opposing team, but stories abound of covert agents with video cameras tucked behind trees or filming from inside their cars, and everyone believes, whether it's right or wrong, that the Raiders have employed spies for years. But even inside the NFL, where people know that spying is real, too much is made of spies at practices. The knowledge a team can gain from watching practice is limited. The spy would have to have such an exceptional understanding of the team and the game that he'd more likely than not be coaching somewhere and not hovering around the periphery of the opposition's practice field.

The best spying by far comes from stealing signals. Teams, some of them habitually, will send out scouts to their opponent's game the week before. Armed with a

pair of binoculars and a notepad, the spy will simply
sit in the crowd, observe the signals being sent in from
the sideline, and document the ensuing play. By the end
of the game, a good spy can have the bulk of the offensive and defensive signals committed to paper, and even
to memory. When a team plays an opponent two times
in one season and the first contest is at home, this for-
mat of spying can be done even more effectively by
filming the signals from somewhere in the stadium and
comparing them against game film to see what play
corresponds with what signal. This of course only
works for the home team who has the ability to put
cameras wherever they wish.

Spying may not always provide explicit answers to
the strategy of every play. However, one team notori-
ous for stealing signals could often determine whether
or not the opposing defense was going to blitz. When
the quarterback broke the huddle, he would look to
the sideline. One designated person would have a towel
draped over his head if the other team's signal indi-
cated a blitz. This way, the quarterback could make an
adjustment at the line of scrimmage to throw a quick
pass over the heads of the blitzing linebackers, or pass
with confidence, knowing that a blitz wasn't coming.

Of course, like every other form of espionage, there
is counterintelligence to deal with as well. One coach I
spoke to used his own spies to find out about the towel
warning for a blitz. When he played that team, he
would signal a blitz in to his defensive captain, but all
during the week he'd prepared the defensive team to
cancel the blitz based on certain passing formations.
The quarterback would see the towel on the head on
the sideline, check to a quick pass, and find himself
throwing into heavy coverage when he thought a blitz
was coming. After the first interception, the towel was
abandoned.

Because of free agency, traitors in the NFL are more common now than ever before. When a player changes teams, whether he's cut, traded, or bought, there is absolutely no loyalty left behind. I can remember one time the Falcons picked up a Rams linebacker who was cut the week before we were to play them. Coaches who pick up players in midseason, and even in the off-season, will almost always debrief the player who was a part of the opponent's team. The information he gives can sometimes be valuable. This particular Rams linebacker gave us defensive linemen all the line calls that the Rams' offensive line used.

He of course knew what they were from years of hearing these calls in practice. If you don't think it's an advantage for a defensive lineman to know when the two buffaloes in front of him are planning a double-team block, you've never played the game of football. That information was quite helpful to me personally, and the rest of the defensive line for Atlanta. There was information, however, that proved useless. They under-estimated this guy's knowledge of their offense, but the Rams, knowing this defensive guy would certainly spill his guts, did change all of their defensive signals and defensive line calls for the game. The lesson is, you can't rely too heavily on secret information, because a savvy team will almost always change signals carried away to another team by a traitor.

The fact that players will so quickly and thoroughly roll over on their former teammates tells you more than anything just how mercenary NFL players really are. But that's okay. Owners, coaches, broadcasters, and even fans are the same way. Hey, all's fair in love, war, and football.

IT'S A MONEY THING

You may hear professional athletes from time to time talking in amazement about how much money they're making and how they'd play the game they play for nothing. You can bet those guys aren't football players. If they are, they're either crazy, or lying. Of course athletes playing games like basketball, baseball, golf, or tennis would do what they do for free. What's the big deal? I would too if I was any good at any of them. But playing football in the NFL is a completely different proposition. Playing football in the NFL is dangerous. I never heard a single guy in my eight-year career say he'd do what he was doing for nothing. In fact, I can't think of a guy I knew well enough to get into any kind of serious conversation with who didn't exclaim that he wouldn't even consider playing in the NFL if the money wasn't so big.

Oh, you might be able to find some insane thugs to battle each other for peanuts the way guys do in those semipro leagues all across the country, and that's fine. The fact is, those guys are more in touch with an element of the game than a lot of the real players in the

NFL. But if you want the world's finest athletes to train their bodies into high-precision machines, endure the grueling grind of training camp and practices, submit themselves to the drudgery of daily mental preparation, and then throw their bodies around the fields of the NFL with the same disregard as if they were so many sandbags, you'd better come up with some serious cash.

This is not to say that the joys of playing in the NFL aren't something that any player would love to have and not need to be paid for. They are. But to get to the point where you are sacking a quarterback in front of seventy-five thousand screaming fans, return that kick one hundred yards for a touchdown, or do a victory dance after throwing a game-winning touchdown, you have to go through hell with your back broke.

Any mentally sound NFL player, hooked up to a lie detector, will tell you that while he may love the game, he's doing it for the money. Don't let someone side-track you on the issue of fame either. In our society, fame is money. Even though, of course, there are players in the NFL who make a measly one hundred and fifty thousand dollars (the salary of a partner in most law firms I might add), even they are playing in hopes of that big free agency payoff.

There's nothing wrong with the way things are. People want to see bigger, faster, stronger athletes, leaping higher, throwing further, and hitting harder than ever before in the history of sports. To do that requires a total dedication of mind, body, and spirit, and a total disregard for one's physical well-being. To get that maximum performance, you've got to pony up. And, considering the entertainment value, it's money well spent.

WHAT ARE SPECIAL TEAMS?

When most fans think of football, they think of either offense or defense. When the special teams take the field during a TV game, that's when you get up to get yourself a sandwich or a beer. Special teams draw fewer viewers than the commercials; no one cares. Yet if you are a true football fan, you should know that many times good special teams will be the difference between winning and losing. A blocked punt or field goal not only directly affects the points on the board, it can change the momentum of the game. A big hit on the kickoff can be as inspiring as a brilliant catch for a touchdown.

If you listen, you will hear almost every coach at every level of the game talk about the importance of special teams. This is because their success is based on how many games they can win, and special teams will usually win or lose at least two games each season. Two extra wins can many times get you to the playoffs.

Many players consider special teams as an unwanted task, something to give rookies and nonstarters so they'll have a chance to participate. But for some, particularly the, well, unusual players, special teams is an opportunity to make the team that they might otherwise not make. When I say unusual I mean of course crazy. Flat-out crazy. Because to be a true special teams player, you have to fly down the field as fast as you can go and throw your body at the opposition like an old sack of potatoes. Every NFL team has at least two players on their roster (besides the kickers) that are there just for their craziness and their contribution to "The Teams," as they're called.

Just as important as having crazy players is having a crazy Teams coach, and I am confident that several years ago the Atlanta Falcons had sole possession of the craziest by far in Keith Rowen. At first I was fooled by his Ph.D. from Stanford, and I mistook the light in his eyes for super-intellect. But no, it was the light of unadulterated nuttiness.

The first time I knew something was amiss was during a punt team meeting. We were watching ourselves practice when suddenly Rambo appeared on the screen in a scene from *Rambo II*. Rambo drew back a compound bow and launched an explosive arrow at his enemy. Rambo's target, an unfortunate North Vietnamese officer, was blown into a million pieces. Rowen was on his feet.

"We're going to blow them up!" he screamed. "We're not going to tackle people on special teams, we won't break down to make the tackle like other teams. We'll throw our bodies around and blow people up!"

"When Jerry came to me," Rowen explained in a calmer moment, "we didn't talk about much football, he just told me that there'd be a lot of prizes for special teams and we were going to have some fun. My contract pays me double when we win, and nothing on the weeks we lose. It's a helluva deal brother, double or nothing, and I grabbed it."

And prizes there were. When you blocked a kick, you got a thousand dollars. The best Teams player each

game got what Rowen called the "Big Meat" award
(dinner at a local steak house). A Bulova watch went to
the second best guy. Everyone who made any big hit
during the game got an official Falcons big-hit T-shirt
adorned with a Falcon displaying bloody talons. The
"Big Lick" award was a ten-pound Hershey's chocolate
bar that went to the player with the most devastating
hit on an opponent. The one prerequisite for winning
the Big Lick is that Coach Rowen hear (or at least
imagine he heard) the "splat" (his word) when contact
was made.

The "Hi-Yukka" award went to whoever went over
the top of the opponent's wedge on the kickoff team. A
Hi-Yukka was when a player literally launched his
body over the four or five opponents who formed in a
wedge and ran full speed up the field to block for the
running back returning the kickoff. This player is inevitably flipped through the air and lands on his back
if he's lucky, or his head if he's not, like a grenade
tossed into a foxhole. The Hi-Yukka award winner not
only went home with a chain saw, he had the dubious
honor of being escorted across the stadium field during
the pregame of the next week's game by a marine color
guard. The player, like the soldiers, would be in full
uniform. Unlike the soldiers, the player had a custom
WWII black battle helmet that bore his name as well as
our Teams motto: HIT THE BEACH. (I think Rowen was a
marine in a past life.) I swear I heard at least one player
who had the honor of the marine escort say, "That's it
for me, man. I actually had to walk across the field
with this thing on my head. There's people out there.
Uh-uh, I ain't makin' no more big hits."

Rowen had a universal respect for big hits and great
Teams players. If one of our guys got laid out by an opponent, Rowen paid his homage by sending the bad
guy on the other team the window shade award. It was

just that, a window shade, symbolic in the mind of Coach Rowen, he told me, of some long-ago Looney Tunes cartoon where the coyote, or maybe Elmer Fudd, got wrapped up in the violent snap of a window shade. As I said, special teams requires, well . . . let's just call them . . . special people.

THE FALL

Most NFL players like to spend the first few months of their off-season relaxing in some exotic place. I spent my time in cold, snowy Syracuse, New York, working on a law degree. I admit it may seem crazy. After all, if you play in the NFL, you certainly don't need to ever work again, right? So what was I doing trudging through the slush with a load of law books under my arm? I could have been on the beach in St. Thomas.

A reporter once asked me, "What motivates you?"

He was baffled when I replied simply, "Fear."

I was afraid not only of what would happen to my bank account, but what would happen to me emotionally when the time came that I had to buy a ticket to get into an NFL stadium.

I think one of the worst things in the world to be is an ex-jock. Actually it's pitiful. I can "be" an attorney until the day I die, but I can't "be" a football player. You either play football or you do not play football. It's something you can only do, not be. It can't last. That's why I was afraid. For the first thirty years of my life I was a football player. It gave me an identity when I was an adolescent, paid for college in my early adulthood, and then as a husband and a parent, it was my livelihood. I came to depend on it whether I liked it or not. And that was dangerous because one day for me, like everyone, it all ended.

But thinking of the future isn't what athletics is all about. In football, players are vaguely aware that each play could be their last, but they're not encouraged to look past next season. Coaches tell players to take things one game at a time, and most don't particularly appreciate post-football plans that distract from the task at hand, winning football games. Most teams now require their players to stay in town during the off-season so they can work on football year-round.

Players aren't supposed to be afraid of anything either. They're big and tough and they just don't lean over to their buddy in the next locker and say, "Hey Joe, I gotta tell you, what really scares me is . . ."

Our entire country is littered with ex-jocks who were never afraid. Some are street bums, some lead what you'd call average lives, some are a tremendous success in business. But they all probably look back and long for those days of fame and glory. It's pretty tough to match the excitement and thrill of playing in the NFL. Let's say you're a lawyer and you win a big case, chances are you won't have seventy-thousand fans cheering for you. Or if you're salesperson of the month, odds have it you won't get asked for your autograph in the checkout line of the grocery store.

I saw the end of football as kind of like a cliff that I would either jump or be pushed off of. It's not that there's no hope. You can do other productive and satisfying things that act like parachutes to break the fall.

But whatever you do, sooner or later you're going to have to take that leap and things will never be quite the same. The problem is, most guys don't even see it coming.

THE SECOND DEATH

They say that football players die two deaths. The first death comes when their career finally ends. My career has ended. No more cleats, no more banging helmets, no more cheers, no more headaches. Instead of the stress and worry of an impending football season, the notion of autumn is nothing more than brilliantly colored orange trees, just like in the postcards. I hear stories in the news about my former teammates losing weight in the heat, having last-minute battles over their contracts, getting injured.

Me? I'm at my home on a cool clear lake in upstate New York. I get up early and go swimming with my kids. I feel great. In the afternoon we take boat rides. I'll usually pull a couple of cold bottles of beer from the ice chest to knock off any remnant of heat that the breeze and the water haven't already dismissed, gaze at the rolling farmland that bounds the water, and wonder at this dying two deaths business.

Of course, it's easy to feel this way now. Training camp is the misery of the NFL experience. But what happens in a few weeks, when this training camp thing is over and the Sunday games begin? I keep telling myself and all my friends that even these games, the gems of the NFL experience, I don't miss. After all, I'm in the broadcast booth for FOX, and still a part of the show.

But who am I really kidding? As great as it is to stay close to this game, to talk about it, to be there watching, to get excited about doing television broadcasts, it really isn't quite the same, is it? I mean, why is it that so many people will sit down to watch those games on TV, go to the stadiums, yell and scream, laugh and cry? It's the game . . . There is nothing like it. It's the most grueling, challenging sport there is. Brute strength, cunning speed, gut-wrenching endurance are all wrapped up into one fast-paced, hard-hitting uproar.

So, the other day I was having lunch at this little coffee shop in town and a young boy came up to me holding out a football trading card.

"Are you Tim Green?" he asked, "the football player?"

I wiped my mouth, then smiled as I took the small child's card and pen. On its face was me, dressed in heavy pads and a black helmet. My arms, where they showed, were glazed with sweat. My face was contorted and my muscles rippling in a frozen moment of exertion. I looked big and strong and even ferocious. I felt that pocket around my heart filling with adrenaline.

"I used to play football," I heard myself say to the boy as I scratched out my name. As I handed the card back to that boy I took one more fleeting look at the image of myself, the ferocious one, and realized that I would never be that again, never be that football player. And in that moment, with those words, I think I died my first death.

More Dreams

As a boy, I'd come in from outside on a cool autumn Sunday afternoon and find my dad planted in front of the TV watching NFL football. How could I fail to envision myself then, heavily laden with pads, sweating and steaming and bleeding from my nose, dressed in an NFL uniform?

Once when I was ten years old, I sat attentively listening to a college coach who was the speaker at our annual Little League football banquet. Having been the starting guard that season on the league's championship team, I was as proud as any boy of ten can be. My future was bright and my dream was alive and well. Then he spoke . . .

"I know many of you hope to someday play high school and then college football. Maybe some of you have even dreamed of playing pro ball."

I nodded quietly to myself.

"But you boys should know this," he continued. "There are about two hundred of you here tonight, and only a quarter of you will ever play varsity ball in

high school. Of those, maybe one, or maybe two, will
ever play big-time college football."

I knew that big-time college ball was a prerequisite
for the NFL. I looked around, critically examining my
competition, searching for the two who might supplant
me. There were several older boys who were much
faster and stronger than me, maybe it would be them.
But our guest speaker wasn't through . . .

"Of the two who ever get to college ball, they will go
into another group just as big as this, two hundred college players. Then, statistics tell us that only two more
from those two hundred will ever play pro ball."

On the way home that night, I was quiet. I clutched
my championship trophy, relishing the cool smooth
form of the golden figure. It disturbed me to think of
the overwhelming odds of my dream. Looking back
now, I have to wonder why. Why would anyone say
something like that to us kids, even if it were true? I
don't know how my fragile child's dream survived that
night. Maybe it was the glint of the golden figure that
sat atop my dresser given life by the street lamp outside
my window.

Whatever it was, I know the spark of that dream
stayed alive. Without that spark, I would not be doing
what I do today. I would not even be who I am. So, it's
easy for me, very easy, to keep the promise I made to
that ten-year-old boy on a winter night twenty-two
years ago. If I ever do make it, I said to myself pulling
the covers tight, I'll never tell anyone they can't. When
I play in the NFL, I'll be famous, like Joe Namath.
When I go to kids' football banquets I'll tell them they
can play in the NFL; they can do anything they want to
do, so long as they aren't afraid to dream.

INDEX

DATE DUE

OCT 7 1997			
APR 28 1999			
FEB 18 2003			